The Victory of Christ's Kingdom

BACK TO BASICS
COVENENTAL HOPE

The Victory
of Christ's
Kingdom

An Introduction to Postmillennialism

John Jefferson Davis

Canon Press

MOSCOW, IDAHO

Published in the present format and title by Canon Press, 1996.
Cover design by Paige Atwood Design, Moscow, ID
Printed in the United States of America.

99 98 97 96   9 8 7 6 5 4 3 2 1

Originally published in an extended format by Baker Book House
Company in 1986 under the title *Christ's Victorious Kingdom: Postmillennialism Reconsidered.*

Scripture references are taken from the Revised Standard Version
of the Bible, copyright 1946, 1952, 1971, and 1973 by the Division
of Christian Education of the National Council of the Churches of
Christ in the United States of America.

Library of Congress Catalog Card Number: 86-50836

ISBN: 1-885767-22-6

Contents

Preface

I am delighted that Canon Press is now making available again to the Christian reading public this version of *The Victory of Christ's Kingdom*. As we approach the year 2000 and the third millennium of the Christian faith, it is very likely that interest in biblical eschatology will be increasing. I have attempted to restate in a clear and convincing fashion the important biblical and historical arguments for the postmillennial position, which for much of the previous century was the dominant view among conservative Protestants and which provided much inspiration and motivation for the Protestant missionary enterprise in an earlier generation. It is my hope that this small volume will encourage the reader with a fresh vision of the resurrected and exalted Christ who directs from heaven the expansion of the church on earth and will give encouragement to the broader Christian community as it seeks to be faithful to the Great Commission in our generation.

John Jefferson Davis
Hamilton, Massachusetts
July 1995

ONE
_____

Introduction

Does the Bible teach that conditions in the world will become steadily worse as history unfolds and the time of Christ's return draws nearer? Are Christians destined to minority status, marginal influence in society, and inevitable defeat prior to the second coming? Or does the Bible teach that there will be a remarkable period of peace, spiritual prosperity, and victorious expansion for the church prior to the return of Christ at the end of the age?

Both understandings of biblical eschatology have, at different times in church history, been widely held among Bible-believing Christians. These eschatological questions are not merely idle speculation about date-setting, but presuppose a philosophy of history and an understanding of the lordship of Christ that have practical and pervasive implications for the believer's involvement in missionary outreach, evangelism, and social renewal.

The present work is an attempt to present a fresh examination of the more optimistic of the eschatological outlooks mentioned, the position which has come to be known as postmillennialism. This view, not widely held in twentieth-century America, and now largely forgotten, was in fact the dominant view among Bible-believing Christians in this country during the last century. It will be necessary to clearly define the term *postmillennialism*, clear up some common misunderstandings concerning this position, examine its biblical basis, consider important objections to it, and explore its implications for missionary activity and social reform.

The point of view presupposed in the present work is that biblical eschatology is fundamentally a matter not of calendar but of Christology. Developing an eschatological understanding is not a matter of assembling isolated texts in some artificial scheme, but rather one of gaining a comprehensive and integrated perspective of the sovereign God's purposes for human history. The New Testament's witness to the ongoing activity of the victorious, resurrected Christ, now exalted to a place of universal authority at the right hand of the Father, extending his kingdom through his Word and Spirit, provides the central focus in relation to which other relevant passages of Scripture are to be understood.

What Is Postmillennialism?

The main tenets of the postmillennial position as it was generally held during the nineteenth century can be outlined as follows:

1. Through the preaching of the gospel and dramatic outpourings of the Holy Spirit, Christian missions and evangelism will attain remarkable success, and the church will enjoy an unprecedented period of numerical expansion and spiritual vitality.

2. This period of spiritual prosperity, the millennium, understood as a long period of time, is to be characterized by conditions of increasing peace and economic well-being in the world as a result of the growing influence of Christian truth.

3. The millennium will also be characterized by the conversion of large numbers of ethnic Jews to the Christian faith (Rom. 11:25-26).

4. At the end of the millennial period there will be a brief period of apostasy and sharp conflict between Christian and evil forces (Rev. 20:7-10).

5. Finally and simultaneously there will occur the visible return of Christ, the resurrection of the righteous and the wicked, the final judgment, and the revelation of the new heavens and the new earth.[1]

This perspective is called postmillennial because in this understanding Christ will return after the period of millennial blessing, not prior to it, as is taught in various forms of the premillennial view.[2] While in the postmillennial view Christ is not physically present on earth during the millennial period, he is the active agent and primary cause of the church's victorious advance and expansion, sending forth the Spirit to bless in a dramatic way the proclamation of the Word of God. (The word *millennium* is derived from the Latin *mille* [thousand] and refers to the thousand-year period spoken of in Revelation 20:4-6.)

Some Misunderstandings About Postmillennialism

Since postmillennialism is a position which has not been widely held in recent times, some contemporary authors in their references to it have not given an accurate representation of its true nature and claims. Several common misun-

---

[1] Clarence Augustine Beckwith, "The Millennium," *The New Schaff-Herzog Encyclopedia of Religious Knowledge*, ed. Samuel Macauley Jackson, 13 vols. (New York: Funk and Wagnalls, 1910), vol. 7, p. 377.

[2] For good introductions to the various millennial positions, see Robert G. Clouse, ed., *The Meaning of the Millennium: Four Views* (Downers Grove: InterVarsity, 1977), and Millard J. Erickson, *Contemporary Options in Eschatology: A Study of the Millennium* (Grand Rapids: Baker, 1977).

derstandings call for comment at this point.

In the first place, the postmillennial perspective is not to be confused with nineteenth-century "evolutionary optimism" or some secular notion of progress. This eschatological view came to prominence among Puritan churchmen in seventeenth-century England long before the Darwinian theory of evolution made its impact in the Western world. According to the postmillennial outlook, any amelioration of social evils is not the result of immanent forces at work within history, nor primarily of merely human effort, but essentially is the result of the supernatural influence of the ascended Christ through his Word and Spirit, working through his people. A spiritually revitalized church is understood to have an increasingly positive impact on the surrounding world and its structures through its preaching, social ministry, and the example of its own inner life.

In the second place, postmillennialism is not to be identified with liberalism or the "social gospel." As will be shown, this eschatological perspective arose within an orthodox theological context, and in nineteenth-century America was espoused by notable conservative theologians such as Charles Hodge, A. A. Hodge, Robert L. Dabney, W. G. T. Shedd, A. H. Strong, and Benjamin B. Warfield.

The postmillennial vision of the spreading kingdom of Christ not only energized the great nineteenth-century efforts in home and foreign missions, but also from 1815 onward motivated social reforms in the areas of peace, temperance, public education, the abolition of slavery, and concern for the poor.[3] There was a widespread conviction during this period that the advancing kingdom of Christ required

---

[3] Timothy L. Smith, "Righteousness and Hope: Christian Holiness and the Millennial Vision in America, 1800-1900," *American Quarterly* 31:1 (1979): 21. See also *Revivalism and Social Reform in Mid-Nineteenth-Century America* (Nashville: Abingdon, 1957) by the same author, especially chapters 5, 10, and 14.

not only personal regeneration but also efforts to redeem and transform unrighteous social structures.

As the nineteenth century wore on, however, many of the theological underpinnings of the original postmillennial outlook were eroded in the more liberal wings of American Protestantism. An early "social gospeller" such as Washington Gladden (1836-1918) still insisted on personal regeneration as a fundamental precondition for lasting social change, but with later leaders in the social gospel movement such as Josiah Strong (1847-1916) this classic evangelical tenet receded in importance. As historian Jean B. Quandt has observed with Strong, "Christ . . . the giver of grace and the lord of history became Christ the teacher and example. Conversion was replaced by moral effort."[4]

For Lyman Abbott (1835-1922), a Congregational minister and leader in the social-gospel movement, the kingdom of God would come through immanent historical forces and institutions: schools, science, legislation, the press, and the churches. The kingdom that was to be ushered in by fresh outpourings of the Holy Spirit was, in the later, secularized versions of postmillennialism in the social-gospel movement, replaced by advances in knowledge, culture, and ethical Christianity.[5] This secularized form of postmillennialism represented in the social-gospel movement has caused some later observers to confuse this eschatological outlook with theological liberalism. The historical record shows, however, that while classic postmillennialism and the social gospel shared a vision for social transformation, their theological presuppositions concerning the nature of sin and salvation were quite different. Historic postmillennialism should not be tarred with the brush of a later theological movement which attempted to reproduce its social fruits without main-

---

[4] Jean B. Quandt, "Religion and Social Thought: The Secularization of Postmillennialism," *American Quarterly* 25 (1973): 396.

[5] *Ibid.*, pp.396, 399.

taining its original doctrinal roots.

In the third place, postmillennialism is not to be confused with universalism, the doctrine that all will ultimately be saved. The postmillennial perspective looks toward a future period of history when the number of those truly converted to the Christian faith will be very great, but at no time does it expect that all will be converted or that sin will be entirely eliminated prior to the eternal state. Postmillennialists do expect a time prior to the return of Christ when a revitalized Christianity will become the world's dominant religion and most powerful moral and intellectual influence, but this is not to be equated with any expectation of universal salvation.

In the fourth place, the postmillennial outlook should not be identified with some version of "manifest destiny" which sees the United States as the key to God's plan for enlarging his kingdom in the world. This confusion has, unfortunately, occurred in the past. In the nineteenth century Hollis Read, a Congregational minister and missionary to India, believed that God's millennial purposes were being fulfilled in America. In his two-volume work, *The Hand of God in History*, Read attempted to show that geography, politics, learning, the arts, and morality all pointed to the coming of the millennium in America. From this base the millennial blessings could spread throughout the earth. The extension of Anglo-Saxon culture and political control over other nations could facilitate the spread of the gospel.[6]

Although God may choose to use a particular nation at some juncture of history in a very strategic way, his saving purposes are not bound to any political state or institution, whether the United States or any other society. American Christians have contributed in a very significant way to the

---

[6] Cited by Robert G. Clouse, "Millennium, Views of the," *Evangelical Dictionary of Theology,* ed. Walter A. Elwell (Grand Rapids: Baker, 1984), p.717.

cause of world missions, and are obligated to continue to do so in light of their abundant financial, educational, and organizational resources. If American Christians fail to rise to the continuing and growing challenges of world evangelization, God will certainly raise up other churches to accomplish his will. The dramatic increase in missionary interest and activity in Third-World churches is seen by some as evidence that this is in fact already beginning to take place.

It should be understood that the postmillennial perspective provides a forecast for the global and long-term prospects of Christianity, but not for the local, short-term prospects of denominations or churches in the nation. Postmillennialists expect that during the special period of millennial blessing the church as a whole will be revitalized, but it is not expected that the pathway in time to that point will exhibit uniform progress on all fronts for all visible churches and denominations. The advance of the kingdom of God against the kingdom of darkness can be thought of as the spiritual equivalent of a world war. The tide of the war as a whole may clearly be running in one direction rather than the other, but this does not mean that the victorious side does not experience setbacks and temporary defeats on various fronts on the way to ultimate victory.

In other words, the merits of the argument for the postmillennial perspective are not to be tied to the judgments about the present or near-term prospects of the Christian church in America. God could send a great revival to the United States, or he could send catastrophic judgment, which will in fact prove to be the case is known infallibly only to God. The point to be underscored is that postmillennialism offers a global, long-term perspective about the future of the church and not short-term local predictions for particular churches and nations.

Voices from the Past

Since postmillennialism is such an unfamiliar position
to most Christians in America today, it is worthwhile to
recall the conservative biblical scholars and theologians of
earlier generations who were committed to this understanding of the Scriptures. John Calvin, one of the greatest leaders of the Protestant Reformation, had an understanding of
the kingship of Christ that paved the way for the full flow-
ering of the postmillennial view in English Puritanism. In
the 1536 preface to the *Institutes of the Christian Religion*,
addressed to Francis I, king of France, Calvin expressed his
confidence in the triumph of the Reformation faith, empow-
ered as it is by Christ the King:

> But our doctrine must tower unvanquished above all the
> glory and above all the might of the world, for it is not of
> us, but of the living God and his Christ whom the Father
> has appointed King to "rule from sea to sea, and from the
> rivers even to the ends of the earth" (Ps. 72:8; 72:7, Vg.).
> And he is so to rule as to smite the whole earth with its
> iron and brazen strength, with its gold and silver brilliance,
> shattering it with the rod of his mouth as an earthen ves-
> sel, just as the prophets have prophesied concerning the
> magnificence of his reign (Dan. 2:32-35; Isa. 11:4; Ps. 2:9,
> conflated).[7]

Calvin's confidence in the spread of Christ's kingdom is
also expressed in his commentaries and sermons. God will
show "not only in one corner, what true religion is . . . but
. . . will send forth His voice to the extreme limits of the

---

[7] John Calvin, *Institutes of the Christian Religion,* ed. John T. McNeill,
trans. Ford Lewis Battles, 2 vols. Philadelphia: Westminster, 1960), vol. 1,
p. 12. The Scripture references in parentheses have been added by the
editor.

earth."[8] Countless offspring "who shall be spread over the whole earth" shall be born to Christ.[9] The Holy Spirit was given to the church in order to "reach all the ends and extremities of the world."[10] Calvin's outlook does not, of course, represent a fully articulated postmillennialism, but it does foreshadow subsequent developments.

It is generally stated that postmillennialism came into prominence through the writings of the Anglican commentator Daniel Whitby (1638-1726), but prior to the publication of Whitby's widely read *Paraphrase and Commentary on the New Testament* in 1703, this outlook was being articulated by Puritan scholars such as Thomas Brightman, William Gouge, John Cotton, and John Owen.[11] On October 24, 1651, Owen preached a sermon before the House of Commons on the theme of "The Kingdom of Christ" in which his postmillenarian outlook is quite evident. That God in his appointed time would "bring forth the Kingdom of the Lord Christ unto more glory and power than in former days, I presume you are persuaded," he stated to the assembly. He believed that the Scriptures foretold a time in history of "multitudes of converts, many persons, yea nations, Isa[iah] 60:7-8, 66:8, 49:18-22; Rev[elation] 7:9," and "professed subjection of the nations throughout the whole world unto the Lord Christ, Dan[iel] 2:44, 7:26, 27, Isa[iah] 60:6-9."[12] Owen, who at the time was dean of Christ Church College, Oxford, is frequently considered to be the most able English biblical scholar of his generation.

The Savoy Declaration of 1658, which adapted the West-

---

[8] Commentary on Mi. 4:3.

[9] Commentary on Ps. 110:3.

[10] Sermon on Acts 2:1-4.

[11] Peter Toon, ed., *Puritans, the Millennium and the Future of Israel: Puritan Eschatology 1600 to 1660* (Cambridge: James Clarke, 1970), p. 6.

[12] William H. Goold, ed., *The Works of John Owen*, 16 vols. (1850; London: Banner of Truth, 1967), vol. 7, p. 334.

minster Confession of Faith to the needs of the Congregational churches in England, incorporated a postmillennial statement:

> according to his promise, we expect that in the latter days, Antichrist being destroyed the Jews called , and the adversaries of the kingdom of his dear Son broken, the churches of Christ being enlarged and edified through a free and plentiful communication of light and grace, shall enjoy in this world a more quiet, peaceable, and glorious condition than they have enjoyed. [26.5]

The Savoy Declaration was adopted by the American Congregational churches in the Synod of Boston, 1680, and in the Synod of Saybrook, Connecticut, in 1708,[13] prior to the beginning of the Great Awakening in 1720. The date of its adoption is an indication that the convictions expressed were not merely an optimistic reflection of revival in the churches, for such revival was yet future for the congregations of New England.

It is well known that Jonathan Edwards, considered by many to be the greatest theologian that America has ever produced, held to the postmillennial outlook. In the context of the Great Awakening, Edwards in his 1747 treatise, "An Humble Attempt to Promote Explicit Agreement and Visible Union of God's People in Extraordinary Prayer," encouraged his fellow ministers to engage in united, sustained concerts of prayer to promote revival consistent with the coming of Christ's kingdom. The main fulfillment "of those prophecies, that speak of the glorious advancement of Christ's kingdom on earth, is still to come," he wrote. There were good reasons to hope that "that work of God's Spirit will begin in a little time, which in the progress of it will

---

[13] Philip Schaff, ed., *The Creeds of Christendom*, 6th ed., 3 vols. (reprinted.; Grand Rapids: Baker, 1983), vol. 3, p. 723.

overthrow the Kingdom of Antichrist, and in its issue destroy Satan's visible kingdom on earth."[14] The progress of the Great Awakening in New England led Edwards to believe that the latter-day glory of the church spoken of in the prophets could be drawing near.

The postmillennial hope represented by Edwards did not die in America with the passing of the Great Awakening; it was strongly represented, for example, in the nineteenth-century Princetonian tradition of Archibald Alexander, J. A. Alexander, and the Hodges.[15] In his *Systematic Theology*, Charles Hodge wrote that the "common doctrine of the Church . . . is that the conversion of the world, the restoration of the Jews, and the destruction of Antichrist are to *precede* the second coming of Christ, which event will be attended by the general resurrection of the dead, the final judgement, the end of the world, and the consummation of the Church."[16]

What Hodge termed the "common doctrine of the Church" was at least the dominant view in the nineteenth century. In 1859 the influential theological quarterly, the *American Theological Review*, could assert without fear of contradiction that postmillenialism was the "commonly received doctrine" among American Protestants.[17] Theologians in the South such as Dabney and James Henley Thornwell, Shedd of Union Seminary in New York, the Baptist theolo-

---

[14] *The Works of Jonathan Edwards,* vol. 5, Stephen J. Stein, ed., *Apocalyptic Writings* (New Haven: Yale University Press, 1977), pp. 335, 412. This volume also contains Edwards's postmillennial interpretation of the Book of Revelation.

[15] See Greg Bahnsen, "The Prima Facie Acceptability of Postmillennialism," *Journal of Christian Reconstruction* 3:2 (1976-77): 48-105, for a good survey of this position in church history.

[16] Charles Hodge, *Systematic Theology,* 3 vols. (1872-73; Grand Rapids: Eerdmans, 1968), p. 861. Italics added.

[17] Cited by James H. Moorhead, "The Erosion of Postmillennialism in American Religious Thought, 1865-1925," *Church History* 53:1 (1984): 61.

gian A. H. Strong, and Patrick Fairbairn in Scotland were all of this persuasion.[18]

The postmillennial perspective of Old Princeton was continued in the work of Warfield, who was professor of theology at Princeton from 1887 to 1921. In an article on "The Prophecies of St. Paul," Warfield gives special attention to 1 Corinthians 15:20-28 and its statements about the resurrected Christ and his continuing conquests in history:

> It is immediately seen to open to us the nature of the whole dispensation in which we are living, and which stretches from the First to the Second Advent, as a period of advancing conquest on the part of Christ. During its course He is to conquer "every rulership and every authority and power" (verse 24), and "to place all His enemies under His feet" (verse 25), and it ends when His conquests complete themselves by the subjugation of the "last enemy," death. We purposely say, period of "conquest," rather than of "conflict," for the essence of Paul's representation is not that Christ is striving against evil, but progressively (*eskatos*, verse 26) overcoming evil, throughout this period.[19]

According to Warfield, 1 Corinthians 15:20-28 depicts the risen Christ as engaged in a victorious campaign of warfare against all spiritual opposition, a campaign in which only death itself—the "last enemy"—remains to be defeated at the second advent and general resurrection, understood as coterminous events. Conservative Christians in this Century have relied heavily on Warfield's masterful defenses of biblical inspiration, but have generally overlooked this aspect of

---

[18] See Bahnsen, "The Prima Facie Acceptability of Postmillennialism." Fairbairn's views are expressed in *The Interpretation of Prophecy* (1856; London: Banner of Truth, 1964), especially pp. 442-93.

[19] Benjamin B. Warfield, *Biblical and Theological Studies*, ed. Samuel G. Craig (Philadelphia: Presbyterian and Reformed, 1952), p. 485. The essay originally appeared in 1886.

his exegesis and eschatology.

By the end of the First World War the postmillennial position was in eclipse with premillennial and amillennial views gaining the ascendancy. The pessimism and disillusionment engendered by wartime conditions contributed heavily to the demise of the once-dominant view in American Christianity. The optimistic and hopeful outlook of the postmillennial vision no longer seemed suited to the times. It has, however, been maintained by a few conservative writers in this century such as Loraine Boettner and J. Marcellus Kik,[20] and also by R. J. Rushdoony, Greg Bahnsen, Gary North, and David Chilton.[21]

In a recent article Stanley N. Gundry argued the intriguing thesis that changes in the dominant eschatological positions over the course of church history had as much to do with the changing social climate as with purely exegetical considerations. Gundry suggested that optimistic periods of history favored postmillenial orientations, while premillennialism gained in favor during periods of historical turbulence and pessimism.[22] Could it be that while premillennial-

----

[20] Loraine Boettner, *The Millennium* (Philadelphia: Presbyterian and Reformed, 1957); J. Marcellus Kik, *An Eschatology of Victory* (Nutley, N.J.: Presbyterian and Reformed, 1971).

[21] Rushdoony and his followers are exponents of the so-called theonomic outlook, which argues for the abiding validity and applicability of the criminal sanctions of the Mosaic law. It should be noted that while these "theonomists" are postmillennialist , not all postmillennialists are theonomists; the two positions are logically distinct. Owen, for example, in a 1652 sermon on "Christ's Kingdom and the Magistrate's Power," clearly distinguished the moral and civil components of the Mosaic legislation in terms of their contemporary applicability, holding that only the moral component is "everlastingly binding." *The Works of John Owen*, vol. 8, p. 394. David Chilton's *Paradise Restored* (Tyler, Tex.: American Bureau for Economic Research, 1984) is an exposition of Revelation from a postmillennial standpoint.

[22] Stanley N. Gundry, "Hermeneutics or *Zeitgeist* as the Determining Factor in the History of Eschatologies?" *Journal of the Evangelical Theological Society* 20:1 (1977): 45-55.

ists and postmillennialists have read the same Bible, one group has focused on the shadows and the other on the light? In any case, it is a rather notable fact that an impressive body of conservative, orthodox Bible scholars—Owen, Edwards, the Hodges, Strong, Shedd, Fairbairn, and Warfield, among others—was convinced by study of the Scriptures that the Kingdom church is to make dramatic progress in the world prior to the coming of Christ. What is the biblical basis for such a hope? It is to an examination of specific Old and New Testament texts that we now turn.

TWO

The Witness of the Old Testament

"Christianity . . . shall not only overcome all opposition, but overtop all competition; it shall be exalted above the hills." This comment on Isaiah 2:2 by Matthew Henry was typical of the optimistic outlook of earlier generations of evangelical biblical scholars. What other strands of Old Testament thought led such godly and learned students of Scripture to maintain such a hopeful outlook on the prospects for the advance of the Christian faith in the world? As we shall see, there is indeed a biblical basis for the vision of the advancing, victorious kingdom of Jesus Christ, foretold in the Old Testament and then more fully revealed and actually inaugurated in the New Testament. The two main foci of this chapter will be the Abrahamic covenant, in which God reveals his universal saving purpose, and the messianic promises and prophecies, which reveal the means by which the divine purpose is to be realized in history.

The Abrahamic Covenant

"I will bless those who bless you, and him who curses you I will curse; and by you all the families of the earth shall bless themselves" (Gen. 12:3). In this first revelation of the Abrahamic covenant, God reveals his desire to bring blessings not only upon Abraham and his family, but ultimately upon "all the families of the earth." At times in her history the nation of Israel relapsed into a very narrow and parochial understanding of her role in God's redemptive plan, but from the beginning it was not so. The God of Abraham clearly intended to bring salvation not only to Israel, but through this people, to all the peoples of the earth.

It is difficult to overestimate the strategic role of the Abrahamic covenant in the design of God's redemptive plan. The noted conservative scholars of the last century, K. F. Keil and Franz Delitzsch, rightly note that this text (Gen. 12:3) condenses "the whole fulness of the divine counsel for the salvation of men into the call of Abram."[1] All further redemptive promises were in fact only expansions and closer definitions of that promise of salvation held out to the human race in that first declaration.[2] As the Jewish scholar Umberto Cassuto has pointed out, inherent in the promise of Genesis 12:3 is the concept of the global reach of God's salvation, a theme which would be subsequently developed in the teaching of the prophets.[3]

The term used in 12:3, *mispachah* (families), denotes a circle of relatives, a social unit related by blood, marriage, or adoption. By extension the term can be used of a tribe or a people, as in Amos 3:2, of Israel as a nation: "You only have I known of all the families of the earth."

It is worth noting that the first statement of the salvation covenant speaks in terms of families rather than isolated individuals or nation-states. The heavenly Father, "from whom every family in heaven and on earth is named" (Eph.

[1] K. F. Keil and Franz Delitzsch, *Biblical Commentary on the Old Testament* (25 vols.), *The Pentateuch,* trans. James Martin, 3 vols. (Grand Rapids: Eerdmans, 1949), vol. 1, p. 193.

[2] *Ibid.,* p. 194.

[3] Umberto Cassuto, *A Commentary on the Book of Genesis,* trans. Israel Abrahams, 2 vols. (Jerusalem: Magnes Press, 1964), vol. 2, p. 315.

3:15), desires that the family structure, so basic to human
society and yet now so marked by the effects of sin, should
be a primary sphere for the revelation of the redeeming ac-
tion of his grace. This family emphasis, so prominent in the
Scriptures, has not always been adequately recognized in
evangelical understanding of the plan of salvation.

After Lot and Abraham separate, following strife between their herdsmen and Abraham's gracious offer of the
choice of land to his nephew, God confirms his earlier promise to the patriarch. "I will make your descendants as the
dust *(aphar)* of the earth; so that if one can count the dust of
the earth, your descendants also can be counted" (Gen. 13:16).
The term used for "dust" here is quite common in the Old
Testament, as in Genesis 2:7, "the LORD God formed man
of dust from the ground." Elsewhere it is also used figuratively to suggest a very great number, as in Numbers 23:10,
where Balaam asks, "Who can count the dust of Jacob, or
number the fourth part of Israel?" Even if allowance is made
for Semitic hyperbole in such usage, it is clear that God is
promising to Abraham an immense progeny, a line and number of descendants that far surpasses any natural human expectation. As Gerhard von Rad has stated, this promise of
innumerable descendants is "a primary ingredient in the
promise to the patriarchs."

After the account of the war with the kings recounted
in chapter 14, and the rescue of Lot, God again speaks
to Abraham, who is concerned that he is yet childless. It seems
that God's promises are not being fulfilled. The Lord brings
Abraham outside at night and says, "Look toward heaven,
and number the stars, if you are able to number them." Then
God says, "So shall your descendants be." Abraham believes
God, and that faith is "reckoned . . . to him as righteous-

---

[4] Gerhard von Rad, *Genesis: A Commentary*, trans. John H. Marks
(Philadelphia: Westminster, 1961), p. 160.

ness" (Gen. 15:5, 6). Abraham is promised descendants as numberless as the stars of heaven. Abraham's faith is demonstrated in his willingness to put more stock in the unconditional promises of God than in his own human assessment of the visible progress of God's purpose in the world. This is a healthy reminder and example for present-day students of biblical eschatology. The promises of God in Scripture, and not present world conditions, should be the decisive factor in our hope for the future prospects of the people of God in history.

When Abraham is ninety-nine years old, God appears to him yet another time to confirm his saving purposes: "I will make you exceedingly fruitful; and I will make nations of you, and kings shall come forth from you" (Gen. 17:6). To reinforce the promise, God changes his name from Abram (exalted father) to Abraham (father of a multitude). The repetition of the promise of countless progeny underscores the importance in God's intention of this aspect of the Abrahamic covenant.

The climactic test of the patriarch's faith is recounted in chapter 22, where God calls on Abraham to sacrifice Isaac, his beloved son and heir of the promise. It seemed that God himself was dashing the means by which the promise of many descendants would be fulfilled. But Abraham, not wavering in faith, obeyed God, considering that God is able to raise men even from the dead (Heb. 11:19; see also Rom. 4:20-21). Abraham's heroic obedience was rewarded with yet another emphatic confirmation of the covenant: "I will indeed bless you, and I will multiply your descendants as the stars of heaven and as the sand which is on the seashore. And your descendants shall possess the gate of their enemies, and by your descendants shall all the nations of the earth bless themselves, because you have obeyed my voice" (Gen, 22:17-18). Earlier references to descendants as numerous as the stars of heaven and the sand of the seashore are here combined. The faith of Abraham is to be a means of bringing spiritual blessings to all the nations of the earth.

The statement that Abraham's descendants shall "possess the gate of their enemies" is the promise of spiritual and cultural dominance of the godly covenant people. John Calvin comments on this phrase, noting that the text means that "the offspring of Abraham shall be victorious over their enemies; for in the gates were their bulwarks, and in them they administered judgement."[5]

After the death of Abraham, the covenant is confirmed to Isaac, in language reminiscent of the earlier promises: "I will multiply your descendants as the stars of heaven, . . . and by your descendants all the nations of the earth shall bless themselves: because Abraham obeyed my voice and kept my charge, my commandments, my statutes, and my laws" (Gen. 26:4-5). Similarly, God confirms his covenant with Jacob, demonstrating the continuing validity of the promise to Abraham: "I am the LORD, the God of Abraham your father and the God of Isaac; . . . your descendants shall be like the dust of the earth, . . . and by you and your descendants shall all the families of the earth bless themselves" (Gen. 28:13-14).

From the perspective of New Testament revelation, it becomes clear that the Abrahamic covenant is fulfilled through Jesus Christ, God's Messiah and instrument of salvation to the world. It was God's design that "in Christ Jesus the blessing of Abraham might come upon the Gentiles" (Gal. 3:14). Those who have faith in Jesus Christ are indeed Abraham's offspring, heirs according to the promise (Gal. 3:29; cf. Acts 3:25-26). It is through the Christian church and the gospel Of Jesus Christ that God will bring into the world a body of believers as countless as the stars of heaven and the dust of the earth. The New Testament Great Com-

---

[5] John Calvin, *Commentaries on the First Book of Moses, Called Genesis,* trans. John King, 2 vols. (Grand Rapids: Eerdmans, 1948) vol. 1, pp. 572-73.

mission (Matt. 28:19-20) to disciple all nations is in fact founded on the Abrahamic covenant's revelation of God's will to bring spiritual blessing to all nations. It is God's design in the Great Commission not merely that all nations receive a "witness" of the gospel, but that a countless multitude actually be brought to living faith in the one true God, in fulfillment of the Abrahamic covenant. This covenant is not superseded in the New Testament but, as Paul clearly teaches, provides the essential foundation for the inclusion of the Gentiles in God's saving purpose. The resurrected Christ, himself the great missionary and apostle, stands behind the Great Commission, and through his power and might the promises to Abraham will surely be fulfilled.

The Messiah and His Kingdom

The instrumentality of the Messiah in fulfilling God's redemptive purposes is foreshadowed in the messianic promises and prophecies of the Old Testament. In the Psalms we find clear pictures of a great king, God's Messiah, ruling over a vast kingdom that far transcends the boundaries of the nation Israel.

The Messianic Psalms

Psalm 2, which may have for its historical background some rebellion of a surrounding nation against David or an Israelite king of the Davidic line, has to be read in the light of the New Testament:

"I have set my king
    on Zion, my holy hill."

I will tell of the decree of the Lord:
He said to me, "You are my son,
    today I have begotten you.

Ask of me, and I will make the nations your heritage,
     and the ends of the earth your possession.
You shall break them with a rod of iron,
     and dash them in pieces like a potter's vessel." [vv. 6-9]

Verse 7, "You are my son, today I have begotten you," is quoted by the apostle Paul in Acts 13:33 in an evangelistic sermon in the synagogue at Pisidian Antioch: "what God promised to the fathers, this he has fulfilled to us their children *by raising Jesus;* as also it is written in the second psalm, 'Thou art my Son, today I have begotten thee'" (italics added). According to Paul, Psalm 2:7 has been fulfilled in the resurrection of Jesus. Jesus Christ, the son of David, is now enthroned in the heavenly Zion by virtue of his resurrection from the dead and ascension to the right hand of God. By virtue of his death and resurrection, he has rightful authority over the nations, and has only to ask the Father that they be given to him as his heritage (v. 8). As Keil and Delitzsch point out, Jehovah "has appointed the dominion of the world to His Son: on His part therefore it needs only the desire for it, to appropriate to Himself that which is allotted to Him."[6]

And does the resurrected Christ desire that the nations be made his heritage? The answer is emphatically in the affirmative, as may be seen in Christ's command to the disciples in the Great Commission: "All authority in heaven and on earth has been given to me. Go therefore and make disciples of all nations . . ." (Matt. 28:18-19).[7] The Father's offer to make the nations the Son's possession is realized

---

[6] Keil and Delitzsch, *Biblical Commentary, The Psalms,* 3 vols., vol. 1, p. 96.

[7] "Disciple all nations" is a more literal translation of the Greek original (*mathēteusate panta ta ethnē*) than the more customary "make disciples of all nations." The more literal translation has the virtue of being more in keeping with the Old Testament's witness to Messiah's dominion over nations, rather than merely over scattered individuals within the nations.

through the Great Commission, as the church in obedience preaches the gospel and Christ sends forth the Spirit to empower that proclamation. Those nations that resist the authority of the resurrected and ascended Messiah are in danger of being broken in pieces with a rod of iron (2:9),as was rebellious Israel in the destruction of Jerusalem (A.D. 70).

Psalm 22, another clearly messianic psalm, speaks of both the suffering and the subsequent exaltation of God's Anointed One. After giving a striking foreshadowing of the crucifixion of Christ in verses 16-18 (cf. Matt. 27:35), the psalmist then speaks of the redemptive impact of that suffering on the nations:

> All the ends of the earth shall remember
>   and turn to the LORD;
> and all the families of the nations
>   shall worship before him.
> For dominion belongs to the LORD,
>   and he rules over the nations. [vv. 27-28]

"The sufferer expects," note Keil and Delitzsch, as a result of the proclamation of what God has done for him, "the conversion of all peoples."[8] According to Henry the text indicates that the ultimate outcome of the sufferings of Christ here depicted will be that "the church of Christ, and with it the Kingdom of God among men, should extend itself to all corners of the earth."[9] It is the Father's will that, through the church's preaching of Christ crucified and risen, "all the families of the nations shall worship before him." Such references to "all the families of the nations" need to be understood not only in reference to the New Testament's Great Commission, but perhaps even more fundamentally against

---

[8] Keil and Delitzsch, *The Psalms,* vol. 1, p. 324.

[9] Matthew Henry, *Commentary on the Whole Bible,* ed. Leslie F. Church, 1 vol. ed. (Grand Rapids: Zondervan, 1961), pp. 599-600.

the background of the Abrahamic covenant and God's desire to bring spiritual blessings to "all the families of the earth" (Gen. 12:3). Reading the texts in this light helps the New Testament believer to avoid "minimalist" expectations concerning the ultimate success of the Great Commission. God intends to bring not merely scattered individuals, but multitudes, even nations, to worship at the throne of Jesus Christ.

The universal reign of God's Messiah is foretold in Psalm 72, ascribed to Solomon:

> May he have dominion from sea to sea,
>   and from the River to the ends of the earth!
> May his foes bow down before him,
>   and his enemies lick the dust!
> May the kings of Tarshish and of the isles
>   render him tribute,
> may the kings of Sheba and Seba bring gifts!
> May all kings fall down before him,
>   all nations serve him! [vv. 8-11]

The Messiah's rule is clearly not restricted to Israel. God's Anointed One is to have universal dominion; he is truly "King of kings and Lord of lords" (Rev. 19:16). That universal dominion is already actual in a spiritual sense with Christ now seated at the right hand of God, far above all rule and authority and power and dominion, with all things under his feet (Eph. 1:20-22), and is also in the process of being actualized progressively in history as the church preaches the gospel in the power of the Spirit—a message with divine power to destroy strongholds (2 Cor. 10:4).

Perhaps the most important of the messianic psalms for our purposes is Psalm 110, which speaks of the Messiah's enthronement, and is frequently quoted by the New Testament writers:

> The LORD says to my lord:
>   "Sit at my right hand,

> till I make your enemies
> your footstool."

> The LORD sends forth from Zion
> your mighty scepter.
> Rule in the midst of your foes! [vv. 1-2]

The Lord (God the Father) says to David's lord (God the Son, the Messiah, Jesus Christ), "Sit at my right hand, till I make your enemies your footstool." The apostle Peter declared on the day of Pentecost that Psalm 110:1 had been fulfilled in the resurrection and ascension of Jesus Christ. David, "knowing that God had sworn with an oath to him that he would set one of his descendants upon his throne . . . foresaw and spoke of the resurrection of the Christ . . . . Being therefore exalted at the right hand of God, . . . he has poured out this [the Spirit] which you see and hear" (Acts 2:30, 31, 33). In verse 34, Peter specifically quotes Psalm 110:1 in relation to the resurrection and exaltation of Jesus as Lord and Messiah.

Thus the risen Christ is now at God's right hand, and is now in the process of subduing his foes. "Sitting at the right hand of God is a description taken from the judicial custom of the East and meant not only the highest honor thinkable but also unlimited participation in the world dominion of God. This heavenly act of solemn transfer introduces a new era in world history, the era of the kingdom of Christ over the whole world."[10]

The phrase *right hand of God* is a clear statement of the location from which Christ exercises his dominion. In the New Testament, Christ's being at the right hand of God is uniformly understood in terms of his reign in heaven (Acts 2:33, 34; 5:31; 7:55-56; Rom. 8:34; Eph .1:20; Col. 3:1;Heb

---

[10] *Herder's Commentary on the Psalms,* ed. Edmund Kalt, trans. Bernard Fritz (Westminster, Md.: Newman Press, 1961), p. 429.

1:3; 10:12; 1 Peter 3:22), and not in terms of a physical reign on earth.

Notice also the crucial adverbial particle *till* (*ad*, during, while, until) used here: "Sit at my right hand, *until* I make your enemies your footstool."[11] Christ remains in heaven while his foes are being subdued and until that process is complete.

This temporal reference has important implications for the believer's hopes for the success of Christ's cause in the present church age, prior to his physical return at the end of history. According to Psalm 110:1, Christ does not need to be physically present on earth to subdue his spiritual foes; this he does while still at the Father's right hand in heaven. Christ already has all power in heaven and on earth. As Keil and Delitzsch rightly note, "absolute omnipotence is effectual on behalf of and through the exalted Christ."[12] This invincible spiritual power is now available to the church in its mission to the world (Matt. 28:18-19; Eph. 1:19-20). The gates of hell itself cannot withstand the almighty spiritual power of the exalted Christ. It is this victorious and confident outlook that pervades Paul's understanding of Psalm 110:1 in 1 Corinthians 15:20-28, an important New Testament passage that will be examined in a subsequent chapter.

While Christ is still in heaven at the Father's right hand, God sends forth from Zion (the church, Heb. 12:22-23) his Son's mighty scepter (the gospel, the Word of God), that he might rule in the midst of his foes. Christ's heavenly reign is exercised and enlarged as the church on earth goes forth in the power of the Spirit to fulfill the Great Commission.

---

[11] For further discussion of matters relating to the word until (ad), see J. J. Stewart Perowne, *The Book of Psalms*, 2 vols. (Andover: Warren F. Draper, 1894), vol, 2, p. 292.

[12] Keil and Delitzsch, *The Psalms*, vol. 3, p. 190.

The Prophecies of Isaiah

The Book of Isaiah contains a number of prophecies that are of particular interest in relation to the postmillennial perspective. The first of these is found in 2:2-4, which speaks of the exaltation of Zion in the latter days:

> It shall come to pass in the latter days
>> that the mountain of the house of the LORD
> shall be established as the highest of the mountains,
>> and shall be raised above the hills;
> and all the nations shall flow to it,
>> and many peoples shall come, and say:
> "Come, let us go up to the mountain of the LORD,
>> to the house of the God of Jacob;
> that he may teach us his ways
>> and that we may walk in his paths."
> For out of Zion shall go forth the law,
>> and the word of the LORD from Jerusalem.
> He shall judge between the nations,
>> and shall decide for many peoples;
> and they shall beat their swords into plowshares,
>> and their spears into pruning hooks;
> nation shall not lift up sword against nation,
>> neither shall they learn war any more.

This famous passage is understood to refer to the latter-day spiritual exaltation of the Christian church, which is the true Zion and the heavenly Jerusalem (Heb. 12:22). A spiritually renewed church attracts the nations (v. 2) to the Christian faith by the vitality and depth of its worship, doctrine, and life. The noun *law* (v. 3), as Calvin points out, is a figure of speech which refers to the Word of God as a whole.[13] The pervasive impact of the gospel in the life of the nations produces a state of affairs where warfare and the production of

---

[13] John Calvin, *Commentary on the Book of the Propht Isaiah*, trans. William Pringle, 4 vols. (Grand Rapids: Eerdmans, 1948), vol. 1, p. 96.

its implements cease (v. 4).

Isaiah states that such things are to take place in the "latter days." To what period of time is the prophet referring? As Edward J. Young has pointed out, the New Testament writers apply this phrase to the period of time which began with the first advent of Christ (Acts 2:17; Heb. 1:2; James 5:3; 1 Peter 1:5, 20; 2 Peter 3:3; 1 John 2:18).[14] In this sense, the entire church age, the time between the first and second comings of Christ, constitutes the "last days." The events foretold in Isaiah 2:2-4 have already received limited, partial fulfillment through the church's missionary outreach and positive impact on civilization, and even more can be expected during a time of dramatic outpourings of the Holy Spirit in the life of the church.

It should be noted that Isaiah 2:2-4 makes no reference to a visible, physical presence of the Messiah, as though the second advent had already taken place. Neither is there a primary reference to the eternal, heavenly state since the reference to plowshares implies that the normal processes of agriculture will still be taking place. The "last days" are the period when Christ the Messiah is still at the right hand of the Father in heaven (Heb. 1:2-3), prior to the second advent and the final consummation.

Isaiah 9:6-7 is a famous prophecy of the birth of the messianic king:

> For to us a child is born,
>   to us a son is given;
> and the government will be upon his shoulder,
>   and his name will be called
> "Wonderful Counselor, Mighty God,
>   Everlasting Father, Prince of Peace."
> Of the increase of his government and of peace

---

[14] Edward J. Young, *The Book of Isaiah*, 3 vols. (Grand Rapids: Eerdmans, 1965), vol. 1, p. 98.

> there will be no end,
> upon the throne of David, and over his kingdom,
>   to establish it, and to uphold it
> with justice and with righteousness
>   from this time forth and for evermore.
> The zeal of the LORD of hosts will do this.

The prophet foresees the birth of no merely human messiah, but a truly divine deliverer, as the striking term *Mighty God* (v. 6) indicates. In Isaiah 10:21, this term clearly refers to Jehovah, the God of Israel. Isaiah 9:6-7 foretells the birth and subsequent rule of Jesus Christ, the divine Messiah and true heir of the throne of David.

Isaiah states that "of the increase of his government . . . there will be no end . . . from this time forth and for evermore." Calvin makes the comment that God not only protects and defends the kingdom of Christ, "but also extends its boundaries far and wide, and then preserves and carries it forward in uninterrupted progression to eternity."[15]

To what period of time does the phrase *from this time forth* (v. 7) refer? A natural way of understanding the phrase would be, in relation to the time when the government is upon Messiah's shoulder (v. 6), and when he actually is reigning upon David's throne (v. 7). The New Testament shows that Jesus Christ, since the time of his resurrection and ascension to heaven at the right hand of the Father, has been reigning from the throne of David (Acts 2:30-31, 33-35). The increase of Christ's kingdom predicted by Isaiah has been in progress since his resurrection and will continue until the second advent and the consummation of all things (see 1 Cor. 15:23-24).

The eleventh chapter of Isaiah contains yet another well-known picture of the conditions of the messianic age:

---

[15] Calvin, *The Prophet Isaiah*, vol. 1, p. 313.

The wolf shall dwell with the lamb,
    and the leopard shall lie down with the kid. . . .
They shall not hurt or destroy
    in all my holy mountain;
for the earth shall be full of the knowledge of the LORD
    as the waters cover the sea.

In that day shall the root of Jesse stand as an ensign to
the peoples; him shall the nations seek, and his dwellings
shall be glorious. [vv. 6, 9-10]

In the postmillennial perspective the references to the paci-
fication of the animal kingdom are understood as figurative
references to the dramatic changes in warring human nature
that can be produced by the gospel. Such effects are to be
more dramatically visible during the latter-day glory of the
church. Henry comments that a "generation of vipers shall
become a seed of saints."[16] Frequently in the Scriptures un-
ruly and rebellious human beings are referred to figuratively
as animals: "You brood of vipers" (Matt. 3:7, John the Baptist of the Pharisees and Sadducees); "I fought with beasts at
Ephesus" (1 Cor. 15:32, Paul of his opponents); see also Acts
20:29 and Matthew 7:15.

In that day, when the name of Christ is exalted in a par-
ticularly powerful manner through the ministry of a spiritually revitalized church, the nations will seek Christ and
his gospel, and the crucified One will draw all peoples to
himself (John 12:32) in a remarkable way.

The blessings of the church's latter-day glory spoken of
in Isaiah 11:6-9 are reiterated and expanded in Isaiah 65:17-
25. The intensified period of spiritual blessing produces conditions in the world that are termed "new heavens and a
new earth" (v. 17). This refers to the dramatic moral renova-
tion of society rather than to the eternal state, since Isaiah
speaks of a time when children are still being born (v. 20),

---

[16] Henry, *Commentary on the Whole Bible*, p. 845.

when people are still building houses and planting vineyards (v. 21) and engaging in their earthly labors (v. 22). Paul uses similar language when he says that salvation in Christ is like a "new creation" (2 Cor. 5:17), or again in Galatians 6:15, "For neither circumcision counts for anything, nor uncircumcision, but a new creation.

The conditions of health and temporal peace of which Isaiah speaks in 65:17-25 are not the essence of the gospel, but they are properly the consequences of the gospel when its impact is intensive and extensive in the world. The message of reconciliation with God also produces as its fruit reconciliation between man and man and even with the natural order itself.

It should also be noted that 65:17-25 makes no reference to the Messiah's physical presence on earth. In the latter days God desires to create in Jerusalem (the church) a rejoicing (v. 18), but the realities of verses 18-25 refer neither exclusively to the eternal state nor to the time following the second advent, but rather to the messianic age when Christ still rules at the right hand of the Father in heaven.

Ezekiel's Vision: The River Flowing from the Temple

The forty-seventh chapter of the Book of Ezekiel contains a remarkable vision of a river flowing from the threshold of the temple:

> Then he brought me back to the door of the temple; and behold, water was issuing from below the threshold of the temple toward the east. . . .
>
> Going on eastward with a line in his hand, the man measured a thousand cubits, and then led me through the water; and it was ankle-deep. . . . Again he measured a thousand, and it was a river that I could not pass through, for the water had risen. . . .
>
> ". . . and when it enters the stagnant waters of the sea, the water will become fresh. And wherever the river goes

every living creature which swarms will live. . . ." [vv. 1, 3, 5, 8-9]

There are other references to "living waters" in the Old Testament (Joel 3:18; Zech. 14:8; cf. Ps. 46:4), but Ezekiel's description is by far the most extensive. What is the significance of this mysterious river which increases in such a miraculous way and brings life to all it touches?

The key to understanding Ezekiel's vision may be found in John 7:37-39, where Jesus, on the final day of the Feast of Tabernacles, stands up and proclaims:

> "If any man thirst, let him come to me; and let him drink, who believes in me. As the scripture says, 'From his belly shall flow rivers of living water.'"[17] Now this he said about *the Spirit,* which those who believed in him were to receive. . . [italics added].

On each day of the Feast of Tabernacles, a priest took a golden flask holding about four-and-a-half pints of water from the pool of Siloam near Jerusalem, carried it through the Water Gate, went up the ramp to the altar, and poured it out.[18] The pilgrims who observed this ritual would likely have associated this water ceremony with the eschatological outpouring of water in Ezekiel's vision.[19] On this under-

---

[17] This translation of the quotation is based on the punctuation found in Western manuscripts. See Bruce Grigsby, "Gematria and John 21:11: Another Look at Ezekiel 47:10," *Expository Times* 95:6 (1984): 177-78, and Raymond E. Brown, *The Gospel According to John* (i-xii) (Garden City, N.Y.: Doubleday, 1966), pp. 320-31, who also supports this translation.

[18] See Mishnah *Succah* 4:9, 10 in *Mishnayoth,* trans. Philip Blackman, 7 vols. (New York: Judaica Press, 1963), vol. 2, pp. 339-40. For further background on the Feast of Tabernacles, see George W. MacRae, "The Meaning and Evolution of the Feast of Tabernacles," *Catholic Biblical Quarterly* 22 (1960): 251-76.

[19] Grigsby, "Gematria and John 21:11." p. 177; Brown also points to Exod. 17, the incident of the water from the rock in the wilderness, as another likely Old Testament background for John 7:37-39.

standing, Jesus is here deliberately presenting himself as the fulfillment of Ezekiel's prophecy. In John's gospel Jesus presents himself as the true temple of God (2:19-21), water is associated with the Spirit (3:5; 4:13-14, 23-24), and Jesus sends the Spirit to his disciples (7:39; 16:7).

Ezekiel's vision, then, finds its fulfillment in Jesus Christ, the true temple of God, who, after his death, resurrection, and ascension to the right hand of God, sends forth rivers of life-giving water—the Holy Spirit—upon his people (Acts 2:33, "Being therefore exalted at the right hand of God, . . . he has poured out this which you see and hear"). Ezekiel's prophecy looks forward to Pentecost and the subsequent outpourings of the Spirit during the church age. The imagery of the ever-deepening river implies that Pentecost was only the beginning; God has yet greater effusions of the Spirit in store for mankind. The Spirit of God, poured out in great abundance upon the church and through the church into the world, is destined to bring as yet unimagined blessings to the human race.[20]

Daniel's Visions

The second and seventh chapters of the Book of Daniel contain visions which are directly relevant to a discussion of postmillennialism. In Daniel 2:31-35, Daniel relates the contents of King Nebuchadnezzar's dream, in which he saw a great image destroyed by a mysterious stone of supernatural origin:

> "You saw, O king, and behold, a great image. . . .The head of this image was of fine gold, its breast and arms of silver, its belly and thighs of bronze, its legs of iron, its feet

---

[20] Walther Zimmerli, *Ezekiel 2* (Philadelphia: Fortress, 1983), p. 513, points to a similarity between Ezekiel's vision of the river and Jesus' parables of growth in the New Testament: small beginnings end with remarkably great results.

partly of iron and partly of clay. As you looked, a stone
was cut out by no human hand, and it smote the image
on its feet of iron and clay, and broke them in pieces;
then the iron, the clay, the bronze, the silver, and the
gold, all together were broken in pieces, and became like
the chaff of the summer threshing floors; and the wind
carried them away, so that not a trace of them could be
found. But the stone that struck the image became a great
mountain and filled the whole earth."

In Daniel's interpretation of the dream the image is understood in terms of the succession of earthly kingdoms, and
the mysterious stone which destroys them is identified with
the kingdom of God (v. 44). Elsewhere in Scripture a stone
is associated with the divine presence (Num. 20:8; Deut. 32:4;
Isa. 8:14; 17:10; 44:8; 51:1).[21]

The Aramaic term used only here in verses 34 and 35
and rendered "strike" or "smite" has a Hebrew equivalent
which can mean "clapping the hands" (Ps. 98:8; Isa. 55:12;
Ezek. 25:6). The context of the passage seems to imply a
process of repeated blows,[22] and the vision emphasizes the
completeness of the demolition of the image ("like chaff . . .
and the wind carried them away," v. 35).

As early as Jerome, Christian interpreters have understood the four kingdoms symbolized by the image as the

[21] Andre Lacocque, *The Book of Daniel,* trans. David Pellauer (Atlanta: John Knox, 1978), p. 49.

[22] Albert Barnes, *Notes . . . on Daniel* (New York: Leavitt and Allen,
1853), p. 135. Boutflower points out that Daniel's Babylonian audience
would have been especially impressed by the dream and Daniel's interpretation, since in Babylonian mythology Enlil, the Most High God, was
associated with a great mountain. The implication of the dream was that
the dominion attributed to Enlil was in fact fulfilled in Daniel's God, the
true God of heaven. Charles Boutflower, *In and Around the Book of Daniel*
(Grand Rapids: Zondervan, 1963), pp. 45-54.

Babylonian, Medeo-Persian, Greek, and Roman empires.[23] Jesus Christ is the living stone, rejected by men but chosen by God (1 Peter 2:4) and now the head of the corner (Acts 4:11), who comes from heaven to defeat all earthly opposition. The kingdom of Jesus Christ, inaugurated during the Roman Empire, overcame it against all human odds, and is destined to expand until it fills the entire earth (Dan. 2:35). The picture of the victorious expansion of the kingdom of Christ is consistent with Christ's own parables of the growth of the kingdom (Matt. 13:31-33, the mustard seed and the leaven). Small and unlikely beginnings eventuate in the universal victory of the kingdom of Christ.

In the seventh chapter, Daniel recounts a vision of a heavenly "son of man":

> I saw in the night visions,
> > and behold, with the clouds of heaven
> > > there came one like a son of man,
> > and he came to the Ancient of Days
> > > and was presented before him.
> > And to him was given dominion
> > > and glory and kingdom,
> > that all peoples, nations, and languages
> > > should serve him;
> > his dominion is an everlasting dominion,
> > > which shall not pass away,
> > and his kingdom one
> > > that shall not be destroyed. [vv. 13-14]

In Matthew 26:64, Jesus clearly identifies himself with this

---

[23] *Jerome's Commentary on Daniel,* trans. Gleason L. Archer, Jr. (Grand Rapids: Baker, 1958), pp. 31-32. Modern critical commentators, who tend to assume a second-century, Maccabean date for Daniel, frequently identify the four kingdoms with the Babylonian, Median, Persian, and Greek empires. See, for example, Raymond Hammer, *The Book of Daniel* (Cambridge: Cambridge University Press, 1976), p. 32.

mysterious figure in Daniel 7. After his betrayal and arrest, Jesus says to Caiaphas, the high priest, "Hereafter you will see the Son of man seated at the right hand of Power, and coming on the clouds of heaven." Caiaphas understood this statement as a claim to be a divine Messiah and responded, "He has uttered *blasphemy*" (Matt. 26:65, italics added).

Stephen, the first Christian martyr, also understood Jesus to be the Son of man of Daniel 7. At the conclusion of his discourse before the Jewish leaders, and immediately prior to his death, Stephen gazed into heaven, saw Jesus standing at the right hand of God, and said, "Behold, I see the heavens opened, and the Son of man standing at the right hand of God" (Acts 7:56). In the Book of Revelation, Christ is described as one "coming with the clouds" (Rev. 1:7; cf. 14:14), as is the Son of man in Daniel. From the perspective of the New Testament it is clear that the heavenly Son of man in Daniel 7 is none other than Jesus Christ himself.[24]

Where is the scene in Daniel's vision taking place—in heaven or on earth? Alexander A. Di Lella points out that the Aramaic words in verse 13, "and was presented before him," are the same ones used in the fifth-century B.C. Aramaic story of Ahigar: "I brought you into the presence of King Sennacherib." The idea involved is that of a royal audience.[25] The Son of man in the vision did not descend from God as if he had been an angel in the divine presence, "but rather he ascended or came to God and was brought into his

---

[24] Critical scholars generally deny that the "Son of man" in Daniel 7 is a personal messiah and argue that the figure is a symbol of Israel or the righteous remnant of Israel. See, for example, Sigmund Mowinckel, *He That Cometh: The Messiah Concept in the Old Testament and Later Judaism*, trans. G. W. Anderson (New York: Abingdon, 1956), p. 350. For analysis and criticism of this nonmessianic view of Dan. 7:13, see Boutflower, *In and Around the Book of Daniel*, pp. 55-65.

[25] Alexander A. Di Lella, "The One in Human Likeness and the Holy Ones of the Most High in Daniel 7," *Catholic Biblical Quarterly* 39:1 (1977): 19.

presence."[26] Daniel 7:13 is thus a vision of the ascension of Christ. This understanding is consistent with Jesus' reference in Matthew 26:64 to being at the "right hand of Power" and Stephen's vision of the resurrected Christ now at the "right hand of God" (Acts 7:56; cf Acts 2:33, "exalted at the right hand of God").

The heavenly Son of man—the ascended Christ—is given dominion that "all peoples, nations, and languages should serve him" (7:14). This dominion is now being realized in the church age as the church obeys the Great Commission mandate to preach the gospel and to disciple all nations.

The visions in Daniel 2 and Daniel 7 can thus be seen as different aspects of the same marvelous reality: the expanding, victorious kingdom of the risen Christ. Daniel 2 describes this expansion from the viewpoint of earthly history, while Daniel 7:13-14 points to the heavenly exalted Christ who is directing and empowering the expansion of his kingdom from the throne room of God.

---

[26] *Ibid.* G. R. Beasley-Murray, "The Interpretation of Daniel 7," *Catholic Biblical Quarterly* 45:1 (1983): 49, thinks that the scene takes place on earth, but admits that most exegetes favor the heavenly location.

THREE

The Witness of the New Testament

Christ's monarchic rule 'over all' makes not only all angelic and demonic powers (1:21f.), but also all men—whether they know it and like it—subject to the terms of his dominion," comments Markus Barth on Ephesians 1:19-22.[1] This recognition of the universal dominion of the risen and ascended Christ is a fitting introduction to a consideration of the New Testament witness in relation to the postmillennial perspective. As noted earlier, the postmillennial outlook is not so much a matter of chronology as it is of Christology—a focus on the grandeur and the power of the ascended Lord and the greatness of his power that is available to the church in its mission. Our discussion in this chapter will be organized along the following lines: first, texts pointing to the greatness of Christ the King; second, texts describing the growth of Christ's kingdom; and third, texts highlighting the final greatness of Christ's kingdom.

The Greatness of Christ the King

"All authority in heaven and on earth has been given to

---

1. Markus Barth, *The Broken Wall: A Study of the Epistle to the Ephesians* (Chicago: Judson, 1959), pp. 55-56.

me" (Matt. 28:18). This astonishing declaration by Christ to his disciples is made after the resurrection and prior to the ascension. Prior to the cross Jesus came in the form of a servant (Phil. 2:7), but now he manifests himself as the almighty Lord from heaven. *Exousia* denotes active power, the full ability to do as one wills.[2] The expression *in heaven and on earth* indicates totality and comprehensiveness. Christ here asserts a universal and plenipotentiary authority; nothing could be more comprehensive. "Never did a human army have such resources behind it," writes R. C. H. Lenski. "All the earth is also subject to him, its inhabitants, both friend and foe, and all the powers that are in the earth."[3] It is precisely in the light of this unlimited authority that Christ sends his disciples into the world as the agents of his kingdom, not in the strength of their own human resources, but energized with a divine authority that is his alone.

The gift of the Holy Spirit on the day of Pentecost was a powerful reminder and attestation to the disciples of the Lord's exaltation and power. "Being therefore *exalted* at the right hand of God, . . . he has poured out this which you see and hear," Peter declared (Acts 2:33, italics added). The apostle then cited Psalm 110:1, "The Lord said to my Lord, Sit at my right hand, till I make thy enemies a stool for thy feet" (vv. 34-35).[4] "Let all the house of Israel therefore know assuredly," said Peter, "that God has made him both Lord and Christ, this Jesus whom you crucified" (v. 36). The crucified one now reigns from heaven, sending forth the Spirit for the growth and empowerment of the church.

Perhaps the most sublime description of the risen Christ's

---

2. R. C. H. Lenski, *The Interpretation of St. Matthew's Gospel* (Columbus, Ohio: Wartburg, 1943), p. 1171.

3. *Ibid.*

4. On the use of Ps. 110 in the early church, see David M. Hay, *Glory at the Right Hand: Psalm 110 in Early Christianity* (Nashville: Abingdon, 1973).

exalted authority is found in Ephesians 1:19-23, where the apostle prays that the Ephesian believers might experience a deeper grasp of the

> immeasurable greatness of his power in us who believe, according to the working of his great might which he accomplished in Christ when he raised him from the dead and made him sit at his right hand in the heavenly places, far above all rule and authority and power and dominion, and above every name that is named, not only in this age but also in that which is to come; and he has put all things under his feet and has made him the head over all things for the church, which is his body, the fulness of him who fills all in all.

This magnificent description of the present reign of Christ can be seen as the "heavenly" counterpart to the words of Jesus in Matthew 28:18, "all authority in heaven and on earth has been given to me." A more comprehensive claim for the authority and power of Christ could hardly be imagined.

In verse 19 Paul ransacks the Greek language to stress the mighty power of Christ, piling synonym upon synonym. "He calls it not only great power," notes Thomas Goodwin, "but 'greatness of power,' and not content with that, it is *to huperballon megethos,* the exceeding, superexcelling, sublime, overcoming, triumphing greatness of his power."[5] The power (*dunamis*) of God which Paul stresses is not just an abstract quality, but a reality which is known according to its working and can be seen and realized.[6] The great might (*kratos*) referred to is something overcoming and prevailing. "It is a conquering, prevailing greatness of his power that is able to

---

5. Thomas Goodwin, *An Exposition of Ephesians* (reprint ed.; Evansville, Ind.: Sovereign Grace Book Club, 1958), p. 332.
6. Francis Foulkes, *The Epistle of Paul to the Ephesians: An Introduction and Commentary* (Grand Rapid : Eerdmans, 1963), p. 62.

subdue all things," writes Goodwin.[7]

Paul discloses this astonishing vision of the ascended Christ not as a theoretical theological exercise, but in order to challenge the believing church to appropriate this mighty spiritual power in its inner life and mission to the world. "The Church has authority and power to overcome all opposition," Francis Foulkes rightly observes, "because her Leader and Head is Lord of all."[8]

The same power that raised Christ from the dead (v. 20) is available, through faith, to believers as they obey the Great Commission. Like other New Testament writers, Paul sees Jesus exalted at the right hand of God (v. 20b; Ps. 110:1), with all things under his feet (v. 22; Ps. 8:6), reigning supreme over all the spiritual beings that would oppose the victorious kingdom of God. God has made him head over all things for the church (v. 22). This is the Christ who has "disarmed" the principalities and powers, publicly leading them chained in his triumphant victory parade (Col. 2:15),[9] and who has gone into heaven, with angels, authorities, and powers subject to him (1 Peter 3:22; Heb. 2:5-9).

There is the greatest possible encouragement here for those who go forth in the name of Christ to evangelize the world. The authority and power of Christ are far above every name that can be named (v. 21), far above that of Muhammad, Buddha, Krishna, Marx, or any others that might oppose the Christian faith. The most serious obstacle to the success of the church's mission is not the power of its spiritual opponents, but the church's own weakness of faith

---

7. Goodwin, *An Exposition of Ephesians,* p. 333.

8. Foulkes, *The Epistle of Paul to the Ephesians,* p. 65.

9. On Col. 2:15, see J. B. Lightfoot, *Saint Paul's Epistles to the Colossians and to Philemon* (London: Macmillan, 1882), p. 192. The allusion here is most likely to the common practice of Roman generals returning in triumph, parading the conquered enemy soldiers in chains through the streets of Rome.

and partial grasp of the invincible resources which are hers
in Christ Jesus.

The Growth of the Kingdom

The parables of growth in Matthew 13:31-33 are Christ's
own description and prophecy of the amazing growth and
vitality of the kingdom he came to establish:

> "The kingdom of heaven is like a grain of mustard seed
> which a man took and sowed in his field; it is the smallest
> of all seeds, but when it has grown it is the greatest of
> shrubs and becomes a tree, so that the birds of the air come
> and make nests in its branches. . . . The kingdom of heaven
> is like leaven which a woman took and hid in three mea-
> sures of flour, till it all was leavened."[10]

These images of dramatic growth recall the mysterious stone
from heaven that grew into a great mountain (Dan. 2:35)
and the miraculous river of water from the temple that in-
creased in depth and width apart from all human agency
(Ezek. 47:1-12).

The mustard seed was the smallest garden-variety seed
known to people in biblical times. "Small as a grain of mustard seed" was a proverbial expression among the Jews for
something minute (cf. Luke 17:6, "If you had faith as a grain
of mustard seed").[11] The plant referred to may have been the
Sinapis nigra or "black mustard," which was cultivated to

---

10. These parables of the kingdom are also found in Mark 4:30-32
and Luke 13:18-19.

11. Richard C. Trench, *Notes on the Parables of Our Lord* (New York
N. Tibbals and Sons, 1879), p. 91.

produce mustard and oil.[12] The seed of one variety of the mustard plant is only one millimeter (.039 inch) across.[13]

The varieties of the mustard plant found in Palestine are annuals and shoot up in a relatively short time, high above the other vegetables. In warmer regions and in rich soil they grow to a great size and the lower part of the stalk becomes quite woody.[14] In Palestine the mustard plant can grow to a height of eight to twelve feet.[15]

This parable focuses on the kingdom in its visible growth. "The kingdom," writes Lenski, "is like a mustard kernel because, like it, the rule of Christ's grace among men has a phenomenal growth from the tiniest beginning." This is a growth which continues throughout time.[16] As such, the parable is a great source of encouragement to the disciples' faith. From small and insignificant beginnings truly remarkable growth will surely come.

The parable of the leaven is also an illustration of the growth of the kingdom, but from a different aspect. Here the inward, secret working of the kingdom and its pervasive influence are in view. Leaven is an illustration of the "mighty, all-penetrating force of the kingdom of God."[17]

---

12. J. A. Sproule, "The Problem of the Mustard Seed" *Grace Theological Journal* 1 (1980): 37-42. On the botanical identification of the plant referred to in the parable, see also G. Granata, "La 'sinapis' del Vangelo," *Bibliotheca Orientalis* 24 (1982): 175-77, and G. Pace, "La senepa del Vangelo," *Bibliotheca Orientalis* 22 (1980): 119-23

13. Robert G. Bratcher, *A Translators Guide to the Gospel of Mark* (London: United Bible Societies, 1981), p. 51, on Mark 4:31.

14. Leopold Fonck, *The Parables of the Gospel: An Exegetical and Practical Explanation* (New York: Frederick Pustet Company., 1914), p. 161.

15. Harvey K. McArthur, "The Parable of the Mustard Seed," *Catholic Biblical Quarterly* 33 (1971): 201

16. Lenski, *The Interpretation of St. Matthew's Gospel*, pp. 527, 529, 530.

17. Fonck, *The Parables of the Gospel*, p. 177. "Three measures" involved more than a bushel of flour-a substantial amount.

"Three measures" were evidently a customary quantity for a substantial meal (see Gen. 18:6). Some interpreters have seen the leaven as a symbol of evil (see 1 Cor. 5:7; Luke 12:1; Gal. 5:9). In this view the parable would be an illustration of the "leavening" of the church with false teaching. But this construction is contrary to the explicit words of Jesus: "The kingdom of heaven is like leaven" (v. 33). Christ and the power of his life, death, resurrection, and teaching—not false doctrine—are clearly the point of the saying. Elsewhere in the New Testament the same figure can be used in diverse senses; for example, a lion as symbolic of the devil in one text (1 Peter 5:8) and of Christ in another (Rev. 5:5). The context must be decisive for the proper interpretation in any given instance.

The parable of the leaven, like that of the mustard seed, teaches an optimistic and hopeful message that is an encouragement to faith. It shows, notes Lenski, that "the gospel cannot but *succeed*, and the one work of the church is to preach, teach, and spread it in the world. The parable teaches faith, patience, hope, and joy."[18]

Both parables describe the small and insignificant beginnings, the gradual progress, and the final marvelous increase of the church.[19] "Nor can we consider these words, '*till the whole is leavened,*'" writes Richard C. Trench, "as less than a prophecy of a final complete triumph of the Gospel—that it will diffuse itself through all nations, and purify and ennoble all life."[20] This hopeful vision of the ultimate outcome of Christian mission is consistent with the immutable redemptive intention of God to bring spiritual blessings to "all the families of the earth" (Gen. 12:3).

---

18. R. C. H. Lenski, *The Interpretation at St. Luke's Gospel* (Columbus, Ohio: Wartburg, 1946), p. 745.

19. Trench, *Notes on the Parables of Our Lord*, p. 88.

20. *Ibid.*, p. 90.

These two pictures of the growth of the kingdom formed a striking contrast with the messianic expectations which were common in Judaism during the first century. "One wave of the magic wand was to accomplish everything in the twinkling of an eye," observes Frederic Godet. "In opposition to this superficial notion, Jesus sets the idea of a moral development which works by spiritual means and takes account of human freedom consequently slow and progressive."[21]

Much twentieth-century biblical scholarship has stressed the apocalyptic features of the New Testament. This point of view would focus on the dramatic and cataclysmic nature of the kingdom, and stress discontinuity rather than continuity and gradual progress. The parables of the mustard seed and the leaven are good reminders of the fact that in our Lord's own mind, the kingdom of God is not to grow and triumph dramatically just at the end of history, but is to exhibit an amazing visible growth throughout history as well. The growth of the universal church may not be even in all ages and locations, but nevertheless, growth remains a basic characteristic of the kingdom of Christ—and this is a great source of encouragement and hope of those directly involved in missionary outreach.

The parables of the leaven and the mustard seed describe the nature and the remarkable extent of the growth of the kingdom; the Great Commission points to the means by which that growth is to be realized in history.

"*All authority* in heaven and on earth has been given to me," said Jesus to his disciples after the resurrection (Matt. 28:18, italics added). "Go therefore and make disciples of all nations" (Matt. 28:19).

---

21. Frederic Godet, *A Commentary on the Gospel of St. Luke,* trans. M. D. Cusin, 5th ed., 2 vols. (reprint ed.; Edinburgh: T. and T. Clark, 1976), vol. 2, p. 122.

Lenski points out that here the word *therefore (oun)* has particular force. "It puts all [Christ's] power and authority behind the commission to evangelize the world. The oun shows that what would be otherwise absolutely impossible now becomes gloriously possible, yea, an assured reality."[22] And John Calvin observes, "The apostles would never have been persuaded to attempt so arduous a task, had they not known that their Protector and Avenger was sitting in the heavens, to whom supreme dominion had been given."[23]

To "make a disciple" is to bring a person into the relation of pupil to teacher, "tak[ing] the yoke" of authoritative teaching (Matt. 11:29), accepting what the master says as true out of personal trust for the teacher, and submitting to the master's requirements as right because he makes them.[24] *Mathēteusate* is an aorist imperative. The aorist form conveys the thought that the command in question is actually to be accomplished; it designates an activity that will result in disciples.[25]

The universality of the commission is made clear by the reference to *ta ethnē* (v. 19), "all nations" of the earth. Here "all people groups" or "all ethnic groups" would be a better translation, since for the modern reader "nation" denotes a nation-state, a politically defined entity, rather than a linguistically defined ethnic grouping.[26] Thus, the one nation-state of India is composed of a multitude of people groups,

---

22. Lenske, *The Interpretation of St. Matthew's Gospel*, p. 1172.

23. Cited in John A. Broadus, *Commentary on the Gospel of Matthew* (Philadelphia: American Baptist Publication Society, 1886), p. 593.

24. *Ibid.*

25. Lenski, *The Interpretation of St. Matthew's Gospel*, p. 1172.

26. For a biblical example of this important distinction see, for example, Esther 3:8: "Then Haman said to King Ahasuerus, æThere is a certain *people* [people group; LXX, *ethnos*] scattered abroad and dispersed among the peoples in all the provinces of your *kingdom* [political entity; LXX *basileia*]; their laws are different from those of every other people."

which may be culturally isolated from one another. The presence of a Christian church within a nation-state does not mean that all peoples within that political unit are being evangelized. Christ's command to the church is not merely that the gospel be preached within all nation-states, but that all the people groups of the earth be discipled through his teachings and divine authority.

In the Great Commission, notes Lenski, "we have the fulfillment of all the Messianic promises concerning the coming kingdom."[27] The Great Commission is the New Testament form of the Abrahamic covenant, intended to bring blessing to all nations, and is the means by which that covenant is to be realized in history. The church can go forth joyously into the world with the conviction that its missionary activity fulfills the eternal redemptive purposes of God and will be blessed with the supernatural power and invincible authority of the risen Christ himself who is with his people even to the end of the age (Matt. 28:20).

The hope of the church's ultimate victory over all the enemies of the gospel does not obscure the fact that in history the representatives of Christ encounter fierce conflict and opposition to their missionary endeavors. But Christ assures his people that even the "gates of Hades" *(pulai haidou)* can not prevail against the church (Matt 16:18). "Hades," the unseen world, is here viewed as a mighty fortress, the opposite of the sacred temple of Christ. The expression *gates* (or, portals; *pulai*) of Hades is a figure for the warring demonic hosts that issue from below in order to assault the church.[28] The implication of the text, according to Lenski, is that "hell's gates shall pour out her hosts to assault the church of Christ, but the church shall not be overthrown . . . What makes her impregnable is her mighty foundation,

---

27. Lenski, *The Interpretation of St. Matthew's Gospel*, p. 1173.
28. *Ibid.*, p. 628.
29. *Ibid.*

Christ, the Son of the living God."[29]

The apostle Paul certainly experienced opposition of all sorts during his missionary labors, and yet he was confident of victory because of the spiritual power of Christ that was his. In the context of opposition from false apostles (2 Cor. 11:12-15), Paul in 2 Corinthians 10:3-5 reminds the Corinthian believers that his ministry is not dependent on merely human power:

> For though we live in the world we are not carrying on a worldly war, for the weapons of our warfare are not worldly but have divine power to destroy strongholds. We destroy arguments and every proud obstacle to the knowledge of God, and take every thought captive to obey Christ. . . .

Paul was convinced that the spiritual weapons of his own ministry—truth, righteousness, evangelism, faith, salvation, the Word of God, prayer (Eph. 6:14-17)—had "divine power to destroy strongholds" (v. 4). Today's missionary facing the "strongholds" of Islam, Hinduism, Buddhism, Marxism, secularism, and so forth can have the same confidence.

The apostle Paul was not intimidated "by the number, the authority, the ability, or the learning of his opponents," commented Charles Hodge. "He was confident that he could cast down all their proud imaginations because he relied not on himself but on God whose messenger he was."[30]

"There is no reason . . . for Christ's servant to tremble before any opposition to his teaching, however formidable," wrote Calvin. "Let him persevere in spite of it and he will

---

30. Charles Hodge, *An Exposition of the Second Epistle to the Corinthians* (1859; Grand Rapids: Baker, 1980), p. 236.

31. John Calvin, *The Second Epistle of Paul the Apostle to the Corinthians and the Epistles to Timothy, Titus, and Philemon*, ed. David W. Torrance and Thomas F. Torrance, trans. T. A. Smail (Grand Rapids: Eerdmans, 1964), p. 130, on 2 Cor. 10:4.

put all sorts of machinations to flight."[31]

The apostle knew, like the apostle John, that "he who is in you is greater than he who is in the world" (1 John 4:4). Paul's confidence in the spiritual power of the gospel was no idle dream, for in less than three centuries the Roman Empire was conquered by these spiritual weapons, and the emperor himself had become a Christian. "This war," noted Lenski, "could not lead to anything but victory."[32]

The ultimate source of the church's growth and missionary expansion is the ascended Christ, who *now* reigns over the church and the world from the Father's right hand, and even now is in the process of subduing his foes. This crucial witness to the present, active kingship of Christ is found, for example, in 1 Corinthians 15:22-26, an important passage for the postmillennial outlook. Paul speaks of Christ's active reign in the context of a discussion about the final resurrection of believers:

> For as in Adam all die, so also in Christ shall all be made alive. But each in his own order: Christ the first fruits, then at his coming *(parousia)* those who belong to Christ. Then comes the end *(eita to telos)*, when he delivers the kingdom to God the Father after destroying every rule and every authority and power. For he must reign until he has put all his enemies under his feet. The last enemy *(eschatos echthros)* to be destroyed is death.

Several important questions of interpretation arise here in relation to the sequence of events that Paul describes. When Christ returns at the second advent to raise the dead (v. 23), Paul says that "then comes the end" (*eita to telos*, v. 24), when the Son then hands the kingdom over to the Father. Does the phrase *then comes the end* imply an interval of indefinite

---

32. R. C. H. Lenski, *The Interpretation of St. Paul's First and Second Epistles to the Corinthians* (Minneapolis: Augsburg, 1961), p. 1206.

duration (a thousand years? [Rev. 20:4-6]) between the second coming and the "end," after all spiritual opposition has been subdued? Or is the *parousia* coterminous with the "end"?

In verse 25 Paul states that Christ must reign *until* all his foes have been subdued—a clear allusion to Psalm 110:1, so frequently quoted elsewhere in the New Testament. Where does this reigning and subduing take place—in heaven, at the right hand of God, or on earth, after the second advent, during a millennial reign? Postmillennial and premillennial interpreters answer these questions in different ways.

In the first place it should be noted that in the New Testament "then" *(eita)* does not necessarily imply a long interval of time between the preceeding clause and that which it introduces (John 13:4-5; 19:26-27; 1 Cor. 15:5-7).[33] More specifically, in this very epistle Paul clearly understands the "end" to be coterminous with the second coming: "as you wait for the *revealing* of our Lord Jesus Christ; who will sustain you to the *end (telos)*, guiltless in the day of our Lord Jesus Christ" (1 Cor. 1:7-8, italics added). The "day of the Lord" is clearly the day of the second coming, as may be seen from 1 Thessalonians 5:2, "the day of the Lord will come like a thief in the night." The point is that the "end" does not come, say, a thousand years after the second coming; for Paul, the second coming *is* the end.

According to verse 24, then, we are to understand that the second coming occurs after Christ has destroyed "every rule and authority and power." Christ is now reigning in heaven at the Father's right hand and now is in the process of subduing his foes. This is the point of Paul's quotation of Psalm 110:1 in verse 25: Christ rules from heaven *until* all foes but death itself are subdued; then at the second coming, the *resurrection* shows that even death itself is overthrown

---

33. W. D. Davies, *Paul and Rabbinic Judaism* (London: S.P.C.K., 1955), p.293.

(v. 26, "the last enemy"). Only then does Christ hand over
the kingdom to the Father.

God delegates his kingship to Christ for a definite period, "from the raising of Christ. . . to his parousia, and for
a definite end, the annihilation of the hostile powers," as
Hans Conzelmann has correctly noted. "Now is already the
time of the sovereignty of Christ, and therewith also of the
subjecting of the powers."[34]

Similarly, C. K. Barrett states that there is "nothing to
suggest that this developing reign of Christ falls between the
parousia and the End; it culminates in the *parousia*."[35] As J.
Lambrecht points out, the "sitting at the right hand of God"
in heaven (v. 25; Ps. 110:1) is interpreted by Paul as Christ's
active reigning on earth.[36] The only other Pauline text which
speaks of the kingdom of the Son *(basileia tou huiou)* regards
this kingdom as a present fact (Col. 1:12-13), not a kingdom
to be established after the parousia.[37]

The apostle Paul, then, in this crucial passage opens up a
vision for the church of Christ's ongoing spiritual triumphs
in the present age. As Benjamin B. Warfield correctly noted

---

34. Hans Conzelmann, *1 Corinthians: A Commentary on the First
Epistle to the Corinthians,* ed. George W. MacRae, trans. James W. Leitch
(Philadelphia: Fortress, 1975), p. 271.

35. C. K. Barrett, *A Commentary on the First Epistle to the Corinthians*
(New York: Harper and Row, 1968), p. 357.

36. J. Lambrecht, "Paul's Christological Use of Scripture in 1 Cor.
15:20-28," *New Testament Studies* 28 (1982): 506; see also W. R.G. Loader,
"Christ at the Right Hand - Ps. 110:1 in the New Testament," *New Testament Studies* 24 (1978): 208; Jean Hering, *The First Epistle of Saint Paul to
the Corinthians* (London: Epworth, 1962), pp. 167-68, and Lenski, *First
and Second Epistles to the Corinthians* p. 672 for similar understandings of
the present, heavenly absence of an "millennial insert" between 1 Cor.
15:23b and 24. W.B. Wallis, "The Problem of an Intermediate Kingdom
in 1 Corinthians 15:20- 28," *Evangelical Theological Society Journal* 18 (1975):
229-42, argues for such a premillennial understanding but overlooks the
force of 1 Cor. 1:8 ("end = second coming") in this connection.

37. Davies, *Paul and Rabbinic Judaism,* p. 296.

in a passage previously cited, this text describes

> the nature of the whole dispensation in which we are liv-
> ing, and which stretches from the First to the Second Ad-
> vent, as a period of advancing conquest on the part of
> Christ. During its course He is to conquer "every rulership
> and every authority and power" (verse 24), and "to place
> all his enemies under His feet" (verse 25), and it ends when
> His conquests complete themselves by the subjugation of
> the "last enemy," death . . . the essence of Paul's represen-
> tation is not that Christ is striving against evil, but pro-
> gressively . . . overcoming evil, throughout this period.[38]

The period between the two advents is the period of Christ's
victorious kingship, and when he comes again it is not to
institute his kingdom, but to lay it down at the Father's
feet.[39]

If Matthew 28:19-20 is the missionary mandate, 1 Corinthians 15:22-26 is a "golden text" of encouragement and hope
for evangelical missions. The church does not have to wait
until Christ is physically present on earth to expect substantial victory in the face of its spiritual foes. Christ, the almighty King, reigns in heaven now, and his invincible power
is available to the church in its mission if only believers will
by faith lay hold of the exceedingly great spiritual resources
which are theirs (Eph. 1:19-23). Paul's Christology is the
key to his vision of Christian history, and sharing that vision can energize Christian missions in as yet unimagined
ways.

---

38. Benjamin B. Warfield, "The Prophecies of St. Paul," in *Biblical
and Theological Studies,* ed. Samuel G. Craig (Philadelphia: Presbyterian
and Reformed, 1952), p. 485.

39. *Ibid.*, p. 487.

The Final Greatness of the Kingdom

We have seen, then, the New Testament's witness to the greatness of the King, the resurrected and ascended Christ, and to the dramatic, supernatural growth of the kingdom— both foreshadowed in the messianic texts of the Old Testament. It now remains to note the New Testament's witness to the final greatness of the kingdom—the astounding spiritual harvest that is to fulfill God's global redemptive intent announced in the Abrahamic covenant and the Great Commission.

In John's Gospel, Jesus, looking ahead to the crucifixion, declares, "I, when I am lifted up from the earth, will draw all men to myself" (12:32). This is not a statement of universal salvation (universalism), but it does announce the global scope and comprehensiveness of God's redemptive plan. This language is consistent with the promise of blessings for "all the families of the earth" (Gen. 12:3) and a spiritual progeny for Abraham as countless as the stars of heaven and the sand of the seashore (Gen. 22:17).

The author of the Book of Revelation is given a magnificent vision of the final harvest of God's redemptive work The results are vast indeed (Rev. 7:9-10):

> After this I looked, and behold, a great multitude which no man could number, from every nation, from all tribes and peoples and tongues, standing before the throne and before the Lamb, clothed in white robes, with palm branches in their hands, and crying out with a loud voice "Salvation belongs to our God who sits upon the throne, and to the Lamb!"

This is clearly a picture of those who have been truly saved, as the language of "salvation" in verse 10 indicates and the number passes comprehension. "In every direction they stretch out as far as the eye can see," comments Robert H. Mounce. "As God promised Abraham, they are in number as the stars of heaven (Gen. 15:5) and the sand of the sea (Gen. 22:17)."[40] The fourfold division into nations (*ethnē*, as in Matt. 28:19), tribes, peoples, and tongues (language groups) demonstrates the global reach of salvation, and shows that the Abrahamic covenant and the Great Commission have been fulfilled in a magnificent, super-abundant way. Here is not merely the cumulation of tiny remnants from each people group, but truly the "full number of the Gentiles" (Rom. 11:25), a multitude which no man can number! As God's original promises to Abraham stretched his imagination to the breaking point, so does this vision of the ultimate success of God's saving purpose challenge us to not limit our hopes by human assessments of the present progress of Christian missions.

The New Testament sets forth not only the hope for the salvation of the "full number of the Gentiles" but also for the conversion of Israel. In Romans 11:25-26 Paul writes, "Lest you be wise in your own conceits, I want you to understand this mystery, brethren: a hardening has come upon part of Israel, until the full number of the Gentiles come in, and so all Israel will be saved . . . ." This phrase *all Israel (pas Israēl)* has, of course, been subject to a diversity of interpretations. Calvin took it to mean the church (cf. Gal. 6:16, "the Israel of God"). Lenski and others understand it to refer to the cumulated remnant of believing Jews over the centuries.[41]

As F. F. Bruce has pointed out, however, it seems quite

---

40. Robert H. Mounce, *The Book of Revelation* (Grand Rapids: Eerdmans, 1977), p. 171.

41. R. C. H. Lenski, *The Interpretation of St. Paul's Epistle to the Romans* (Minneapolis: Augsburg, 1961), p. 727; Charles M. Horne, "The Meaning of the Phrase, 'And Thus All Israel Will Be Saved' (Rom. 11:26)," *Evangelical Theological Society Journal* 21 (1978): 334.

artificial to read a meaning for "Israel" in verse 26 different from the sense of "Israel" in verse 25 ("a hardening has come upon part of Israel"). In verse 25 the Israel that is hardened is clearly ethnic Israel, the nation as a whole that has not responded to the gospel. The phrase *all Israel* is a recurring one in Jewish literature, Bruce observes, "where it does not mean 'every Jew without a single exception' but 'Israel as a whole.' Thus 'all Israel has a portion in the age to come,' says the Mishnah tractate *Sanhedrin* (x.i), and proceeds immediately to name those Israelites who have no portion therein."[42] As Franz J. Leenhardt has pointed out, the term *all Israel* forms a contrast with the "remnant" (v. 5); both phrases have clear ethnic connotations.[43] Elsewhere in Romans 9-11, the term *Israel* clearly refers to ethnic Israel (9:3-5; 9:6; 9:30-31; 10:19; 10:21; 11:1; 11:7; 11:25).

Paul thus looks forward to a time when the nation of Israel will recognize her true Messiah and enjoy the blessings of salvation in Jesus Christ. No mention is made here, however, of the restoration of an earthly Davidic kingdom, for what Paul envisioned for his people was something infinitely better.[44]

The closing pages of the New Testament contain a marvelous vision of the New Jerusalem in all its vastness and glory:

> And he who talked to me had a measuring rod of gold to measure the city and its gates and walls. The city lies foursquare, its length the same as its breadth; and he measured the city with his rod, twelve thousand stadia; its length and breadth and height are equal. [Rev. 21.15-16]

---

42. F. F. Bruce, *The Epistle of Paul to the Romans* (Grand Rapids: Eerdmans, 1963), pp. 221-22.

43. Franz J. Leenhardt, *The Epistle to the Romans: A Commentary*, trans. Harold Knight (Cleveland: World, 1961), p. 293.

44. Bruce, *The Epistle of Paul to the Romans*, p. 221.

The church, the New Jerusalem, is depicted as a cube, reminiscent of the Holy of Holies in the tabernacle and the Solomonic temple. The three equal dimensions of the cube are symbolic of spiritual perfection.[45]

Each side of the city is twelve thousand stadia or about fifteen hundred miles long, so that the surface area of the New Jerusalem is some 2,250,000 square miles. In the rabbinic literature there were descriptions of a recreated Jerusalem that would reach Damascus and cover the whole of Palestine, but John's vision dwarfs even those.[46]

The point here is surely that the proportions of the heavenly city, God's church, are incredibly vast. This is consistent with the reference to the "countless multitude" (Rev. 7:9). The ultimate outcome of the church's missionary efforts will far surpass our current human expectations, because God "by the power at work within us is able to do far more abundantly than all that we ask or think" (Eph. 3:20). The New Testament's witness to the final greatness of the kingdom is a constant source of encouragement to the church in its mission. Believing these things, God's people can be "steadfast, immovable, always abounding in the work of the Lord, knowing that in the Lord your labor is not in vain" (1 Cor. 15:58).

---

45. R. C. H. Lenski, *The Interpretation of St. John's Revelation* (Minneapolis: Augsburg, 1961), p. 637.

46. William Barclay, *The Revelation of John*, 2 vols. (Philadelphia: Westminster, 1976), vol. 2. p. 212.

FOUR

Contrary Texts in the New Testament

According to Millard J. Erickson, one of the difficulties with the postmillennial position is that it tends to neglect biblical passages that "portray spiritual and moral conditions as worsening in the end times."[1] There are also many New Testament texts that appear to portray the return of Christ as imminent. Could the postmillennial outlook, which suggests a long period of time prior to the second advent, possibly be consistent with such texts? And finally, what of texts which appear to teach that the number of the faithful will be small when Christ returns (e.g., Luke 18:8, "When the Son of man comes, will he find faith on earth?")?

Any viable eschatological framework must take into account all the relevant biblical data. This chapter will attempt to show how the types of texts mentioned are understood within a postmillennial framework.

"Behold, the Judge Is Standing at the Doors"

The New Testament contains many passages which express a sense of the nearness of the return of Christ. This

---

[1] Millard J. Erickson, *Contemporary Options in Eschatology: A Study of the Millennium* (Grand Rapids: Baker, 1977), p. 72.

sense of the imminency of the parousia is the basis for ethical exhortations for the believer to maintain an attitude of watchfulness and spiritual alertness. "Watch therefore, for you do not know on what day your Lord is coming. . . . Therefore you also must be ready, for the Son of man is coming at an hour you do not expect" (Matt. 24:42, 44). Such an awareness of the nearness of the end is also pervasive in the Epistles. Paul writes to the Christians in Rome that "salvation is nearer to us now than when we first believed; the night is far gone, the day is at hand" (Rom. 13:11-12). Marriage may be inexpedient for some in Corinth, since "the appointed time has grown very short" (1 Cor. 7:29). In his first letter to the Thessalonian church, the apostle appears to include himself among those who will still be alive at the time of the advent: "we who are alive, who are left until the coming of the Lord, shall not precede [in the rapture] those who have fallen asleep" (1 Thess. 4:15).[2]

This sense of imminency can also be seen in the general Epistles. James warns the community not to grumble against one another, in order to avoid Christ's judgment, inasmuch as "the Judge is standing at the doors" (James 5:9). Peter exhorts the Christians in Asia Minor to keep sane and sober for prayer since "the end of all things is at hand" (1 Peter 4:7). The Johannine community is warned about the coming of false teachers, whose very presence is evidence that it is the "last hour" (1 John 2:18).

The closing lines of the Apocalypse contain the promise of the risen Christ, "Surely I am coming soon" (Rev. 22:20).

---

[2] On the question of development over time in Paul's eschatology, see Richard N. Longenecker, "The Nature of Paul's Early Eschatology," *New Testament Studies* 31(1985): 85-95. Longenecker does see some development in Paul's eschatology, but argues that the apostle's primary commitment "was not first of all to a program or some timetable of events but to a person: Jesus the Messiah" (p. 93). In other words, the primary emphasis of Pauline eschatology is christological, not calendrical.

There are various ways in which the interpreter of Scripture can respond to this sense of imminency expressed in texts that are now almost two thousand years old. Some scholars have concluded that Jesus and/or his followers were simply mistaken on the question of the time of the second advent, a mistake that is understandable given the limitations of human nature and historical circumstances.[3] Others have suggested that the belief in an imminent parousia may have been produced by the (mistaken) activity of itinerant prophets in the early church.[4] It has also been argued that the parousia already took place in A.D. 70 when, through the instrumentality of the Roman armies, Christ came spiritually in judgment upon Jerusalem. The New Testament texts have reference to this event, and not to some yet future advent.[5]

These approaches are not consistent with the evangelical tradition of interpretation as generally understood, and do not appear to be required by the texts themselves. A more adequate approach to the question of the imminency of the parousia and its bearing on the postmillennial understanding would include a variety of different considerations, the more important of which include the following:

First, God's perspective on time is not the same as our own, as 2 Peter 3:8 makes clear: "with the Lord one day is as a thousand years, and a thousand years as one day." The allusion here is to Psalm 90:4, a psalm which contrasts God's eternity and man's transience. The apparent delay in Christ's parousia is actually an expression of God's mercy, for he

---

[3] See, for example, H. P. Owen, "The Parousia of Christ in the Synoptic Gospels," *Scottish Journal of Theology* 12 (1959): 171-92.

[4] J. G. Davies, "The Genesis of Belief in an Imminent Parousia," *Journal of Theological Studies* n.s. 14 (1963). 104-7.

[5] J. Stuart Russell, *The Parousia: A Study of the New Testament Doctrine of Our Lord's Second Coming* (reprint ed.; Grand Rapids: Baker 1983).

wished that even the scoffers (v. 3) would reach repentance.[6] From God's point of view, the span between the first century and our own is only several "days," and God in his mercy may well ordain many more such "days" in the future to complete his purpose of bringing the gospel of repentance to all.

Second, there is the phenomenon in Scripture that has been termed "telescoping" or "compression" of immediate historical judgments and the ultimate judgment which they prefigure. The prophet Joel, on the occasion of a locust plague devastating Judah (Joel 1:4), states that "the day of the LORD is coming, it is near" (2:1). Some twenty-five hundred years later, the ultimate judgment is yet to come. Evidently the prophet saw in the locust plague a prefiguring of the final judgment.' and the two events are superimposed in his outlook.[7] The reality and certainty of impending divine judgment are expressed in the existential sense of "nearness." A similar phenomenon may be observed in Isaiah 61:2, where the prophet compresses the first and second advent. The

---

[6] Charles H. Talbert, "II Peter and the Delay of the Parousia," *Vigilae Christianae* 20 (1966): 137-45, has perceptively pointed out that nowhere does the author say that the whole church was disturbed by a "delayed Parousia," as most scholars tend to assume. Rather, the only ones who appear to consider the delay of the parousia a problem are the heretics, the outsiders (3:3-4). These Gnostics advocated a realized-spiritualized eschatology, and hence were disturbed by the hope of a yet future parousia, a parousia bringing judgment on the lifestyles displayed by the scoffers. Talbert concludes that 2 Peter "cannot be used as evidence for the thesis that the delay of the Parousia caused a crisis of major proportions in the life and thought of early Christianity" (p. 145). See also Richard J. Bauckham, "The Delay of the Parousia," *Tyndale Bulletin* 31 (1980): 3-36.

[7] K. F. Keil, *Biblical Commentary on the Old Testament* (25 vols.), *The Twelve Minor Prophets*, trans. James Martin, 2 vols. (Grand Rapids: Eerdmans, 1949), vol. 1, p. 190: "Joel now proclaims the coming of that day in its full completion, on the basis of the judgment already experienced." The coming of the day of Jehovah is represented as "indisputably certain" (p. 189).

servant of the Lord comes to "proclaim the year of the
LORD's favor, and the day of vengence of our God." Significantly, in Luke 4:18-19, in Luke's account of Jesus' ap-
pearance at the synagogue in Nazareth, the Lord reads from
the Isaiah scroll, but stops at 61:2a ("the acceptable year of
the Lord"), and omits 61:2b ("the day of vengence of our
God"). Christ distinguished his first advent in mercy from
the second in judgment, whereas Isaiah had superimposed
the two. It may be that New Testament texts expressing the
sense of the imminency of the parousia could likewise "fore-
shorten" the time between the ascension of Christ and the
end of all things.

Third, it should be observed that the New Testament
contains not only texts expressing a sense of imminency,
but also those which speak of possible delay. The parable of
the faithful and unfaithful servants (Matt. 24:4551: Luke
12:4246) has the wicked servant saying to himself, "My master is delayed" (Matt. 24:48). In the parable of the ten vir-
gins, the maidens all slumbered and slept as the bridegroom
was delayed (Matt. 25:5). In the parable of the talents (Matt.
25:14-30), it is stated that "after a long time" (v. 19) the master returned from his journey and settled accounts with the
servants to whom he had entrusted his property. Such texts
reminded the early church that the sense of the nearness of
the end had to be held in tension with the possibility of the
master's delay.

Significantly, the exhortations to watchfulness in the
New Testament are predicated not so much on the known
chronological nearness of the parousia as on its unexpectedness; for example, Matthew 24:44, "Therefore you also must
be ready; for the Son of man is coming at an hour *you do not
expect*" (italics added). The day of the Lord will come like "a
thief in the night," (1 Thess. 5:2) that is, unexpectedly. It is
this unexpectedness and uncertainty of the time of the end,
rather than any human ability to calculate its time on the
calendar, which is the foundation for the admonitions to

remain alert and spiritually awake.

Fourth, the New Testament does speak of events which are to precede the end and which imply a significant interval between the ascension of Christ and his final coming in glory The gospel is to be preached throughout the whole world as a testimony to the nations before the end comes (Matt. 24:14; cf. Luke 24:47).[8] While it can be argued that in a sense this has already been accomplished, the gospel having been preached throughout the entire known world (the Roman Empire) in Paul's own day (Col. 1:6), the gospel texts would appear to imply a more truly universal sense of the "whole world." Surely the commission to make disciples of "all nations" (Matt. 28:19) was intended by Christ to extend beyond the boundaries of the Roman Empire, especially in light of the global authority of Christ ("all authority in heaven and on earth," v. 18) that is the foundation of the commission. The mandate is to extend Christ's kingdom throughout the earth, for his authority extends over all without exception. The author of the Apocalypse states that the blood of the Lamb has ransomed men for God from every tongue and tribe and people and nation (Rev. 5:9). A countless multitude from every nation.' from all tribes and peoples and tongues (Rev. 7:9), is seen standing before the heavenly throne, acclaiming God and the Lamb for the salvation that has been wrought. The global reach of such language is difficult to deny and implies a considerable task that is yet to be completed by the church in its missionary tasks.

Fifth, it should be noted that Christ can come at any time in providential judgment upon a nation, church, or individual. In the Old Testament God comes spiritually yet truly in judgment on rebellious nations. In an oracle con-

---

[8] Richard H. Hiers, "The Delay of the Parousia in Luke-Acts," *New Testament Studies* 20 (1974): 154: "Luke . . . makes it clear that Jesus did not look for the Parousia until the gentile mission had been completed: 24:46; Acts 1:6-8."

cerning Egypt, Isaiah says, "Behold, the LORD is riding on
a swift cloud and comes to Egypt" (Isa. 19:1). God was not
physically present, but Nebuchadnezzar did invade Egypt
about 568 B.C., and as such was the human instrument of
the divine judgment. Through the instrumentality of the
Roman armies of Titus, God came in judgment upon rebellious Jerusalem in A.D. 70 and the resulting devastation fulfilled the prophecy of Christ recorded in Matthew 24:1-2.
The risen Christ warns the church at Ephesus that "I will
come to you and remove your lampstand from its place,
unless you repent" (Rev. 2:5). Those at Pergamum receive a
similar warning: "Repent then. If not, I will come to you
soon and war against them with the sword of my mouth"
(Rev. 2:16). The reference to the "sword of my mouth" is
figurative language (cf. 1:16), but the spiritual coming in judgment is very real in its effects. Certain individuals in Corinth
who were abusing the Lord's Supper experienced the judgment of Christ to the point of illness and even death (1 Cor.
11:29-32). The risen Christ who is now at the right hand of
the Father and who will return at the end of history as the
Judge of the world is also the one whose presence is felt in
judgment by nations, churches, and individuals within history. The reality of Christ's spiritual visitations in judgment
in history provides a sober warning to the church to maintain its watchfulness and spiritual vigilance.

Sixth, and most importantly, the sense of the imminency
of the parousia in the New Testament is to be understood in
terms of the reality of Christ's finished victory at the cross
and the powerful presence of the Holy Spirit in the church.
The early church had a vivid sense of the nearness of the end
because, in a very real sense, the final events of the end had
already come in Jesus. In the preaching of Jesus the kingdom of God had drawn near (Mark 1:15). Satan's power had
been stripped away at the cross (Col. 2:15), and the death of
Christ had abolished death (2 Tim. 1:10). The final events
of the end are, as A. L. Moore has pointed out, "already

accomplished in Christ."[9] Furthermore, the Holy Spirit in
the church not only communicates to the believer the reality of Christ's past work, but the presence of the Spirit is a
sign of the end as well, and "an assurance that the present is
already . . . an anticipation of the Last Age."[10] The "first
fruits" of the Spirit (Rom. 8:23) experienced by the believer
now make real the complete redemption of the age to come.
The New Testament writers had a vivid sense of imminency,
but nowhere set dates for the parousia. They realized, as
Moore has noted, that "the time for repentance and faith
could not be limited by men and that the provision of God's
mercy could not be measured or forecast."[11] The sense of
the imminency of the parousia in the New Testament, then,
is fundamentally christological and existential rather than
chronological and calendrical in nature. The nearness of
Christ cannot be adequately understood in terms of simple
linear time. Our normal temporal categories have been col-
lapsed by the cross, resurrection, and sending of the Holy
Spirit. The spiritual realities help us to understand the para-
doxical combination of New Testament expressions of the
nearness of the end and, at the same time, warnings of delay—a delay that is itself an expression of God's sovereign
grace and mercy, and the time of the church's mission.

"In the Last Days, There Will Come Times of Stress"

Is world history "running downhill"? Does the Bible

---

[9] A. L. Moore, *The Parousia in the New Testament* (Leiden: E. J. Brill, 1966), p. 168. Moore's excellent treatment points out the weakness of much recent New Testament scholarship, which frequently tends to assume that Jesus and the early church were simply mistaken in their eschatological expectations.

[10] *Ibid.*, p. 169.

[11] *Ibid.*, pp. 206-7.

teach that world conditions will steadily deteriorate with the passage of time, and that this decline will be climaxed with an unparalleled time of worldwide, violent persecution of Christians ("the great tribulation") immediately prior to the return of Christ? Many scriptural passages have been interpreted in such a sense.

Writing to the Christians in Galatia, the apostle Paul speaks of the "present evil age" (Gal. 1:4). John declares that "the whole world is in the power of the evil one" (1 John 5:19). Jesus warns the disciples that in the world they will have tribulation (John 16:33). In the last days there will indeed come times of stress (2 Tim. 3:1). In the Olivet discourse the Lord speaks of a time of "great tribulation, such as has not been from the beginning of the world until now, no, and never will be" (Matt. 24:21). In the face of such biblical statements, is it possible to maintain an optimistic hope for the future course of human history?

The statements of Galatians 1:4 and 1 John 5:19 need to be seen as realistic descriptions of Satan's continuing rear guard actions in the world. It is true that Satan still prowls about like a roaring lion, seeking someone to devour (1 Peter 5:8). But more fundamentally, Satan's power is a broken power, and his authority a pseudo-authority. Satan has been decisively defeated at the cross of Christ (Col. 2:15). John also confidently writes that "he who is in you is greater than he who is in the world" (1 John 4:4). Whoever is born of God overcomes the world, and "this is the victory that overcomes the world, our faith" (1 John 5:4). Raymond E. Brown observes that "the author means that Christian conquest is inevitable, flowing from the fact that the world has already been conquered by Jesus."[12] Paul may speak of the "present

---

[12] Raymond E. Brown, *The Epistles of John* (Garden City, N Y.; Doubleday, 1982), p. 572. In a similar vein, I. Howard Marshall, *The Epistles of John* (Grand Rapids: Eerdmans, 1978), p. 229, comments, "Such faith is far from being wish-fulfillment . . . it rests foursquare on the fact that Jesus Christ has defeated death, and anybody who can defeat death can defeat anything."

evil age," but this does not produce passivity and resignation in his own ministry or in his hope for the church. He knows that the power of Christ is far greater than that of the evil one. He knows that the spiritual weapons of his apostolic ministry have "divine power to destroy strongholds" and can take every thought captive to Christ (2 Cor. 10:4, 5). Satan has been defeated, and Paul writes to the Christians in Rome that "the God of peace will soon crush Satan under your feet" (Rom. 16:20). This is hardly the voice of historical pessimism!

It is indeed true that in the world Christians experience tribulation (John 16:33; Rom. 8:35), as the history of the church has attested. But tribulation is not to be identified with defeat of Christ's cause on earth. Tribulation there may be, but Christ has overcome the world (John 16:33b). Those who are called to martyrdom in fact conquer the evil one by the blood of the Lamb and by the word of their testimony (Rev. 12:11).

Will tribulation, especially in the sense of bloody persecution, intensify as the end draws near? Is this the sense of 2 Timothy 3:1, "in the last days there will come times of stress"? With respect to this text, several observations are in order. First, Paul states that the ungodly behavior that is to be prominent in the end time is already apparent; Timothy is warned to "avoid" the ungodly (2 Tim. 3:5). The church is already living in the end time, which extends from the resurrection of Christ to the parousia (cf. Heb. 1:2, "in these last days"), and such times of "stress" are manifested in various degrees of intensity throughout the church age.

Second, it is significant that there is nowhere in 2 Timothy 3:1-8 any explicit mention of violent persecution of Christians. Burton Scott Easton notes that "overt crimes are omitted from the list of vices, and nothing is said about physical woes' such as eclipses, earthquakes, pestilence," and so forth.[13] Rather, the characteristic features of the time appear to be hedonism, materialism, egotism, and hypocrisy in religion: "lovers of self, lovers of money . . . lovers of pleasure rather than lovers of God, holding the form of religion but denying the power of it" (vv. 2, 4-5). This picture is quite consistent with Christ's description of worldly conditions immediately prior to the end (Luke 17:26-30). During the days of Noah and of Lot, the picture was one of apparent normalcy: eating, drinking, marrying, giving in marriage, buying, selling, planting, building (vv. 27-28)—but then sudden judgment came. This picture of a careless and complacent generation of unbelievers immediately prior to the parousia is given as well by Paul in 1 Thessalonians 5:3: "When people say, 'There is *peace and security*,' then sudden destruction will come upon them . . . and there will be no escape" (italics added). Leon Morris notes that the present tense of *legōsin* in verse 3 indicates that "they will still be saying words at the very moment when the 'sudden destruction' comes."[14]

These three texts (2 Tim. 3:1-5; Luke 17:26-30; and 1 Thess. 5:3) teach, then, that immediately prior to the parousia the church is not to look so much for "war and rumors of wars," great violent persecution, and social turmoil, but rather for the more insidious spiritual threat of complacency, worldliness, materialism, and hedonism.[15] A postmillennial framework can incorporate these texts, inasmuch as within this framework there is a final apostasy and deceiving of the

---

[13] Burton Scott Easton, *The Pastoral Epistles* (London: SCM, 1948), p. 63. Martin Dibelius and Hans Conzelmann, *The Pastoral Epistles: A Commentary on the Pastoral Epistles*, ed. Helmut Koester, trans. Philip Buttolph and Adela Yarbro (Philadelphia: Fortress, 1972), p. 116, note that the list of vices "is in many ways reminiscent of Rom. 1:30f."

[14] Leon Morris, *The First and Second Epistles to the Thessalonians* (Grand Rapids: Eerdmans, (1959), p. 153.

[15] Likewise, in 2 Thess. 1:1-11, the great threat to the church is not overt persecution, but wicked deception (v. 10) inspired by Satan himself: the threat of false religion.

nations (Rev. 20:7-8; 2 Thess. 2:9-11) immediately prior to the second advent and after the period of millennial blessing on the church (Rev. 20:4-6). Indeed, the very conditions of temporal prosperity which are a secondary effect of the millennial blessings make the worldliness and carelessness described in 2 Timothy 3:1-5, Luke 17:26-30, and 1 Thessalonians 5:3 understandable but not excusable. Vast numbers of nominal believers and professing unbelievers grow proud and careless because of their worldly prosperity, and even the church is sorely tested by conditions of affluence in the millennial period. Church history and the experience of Christians in Europe and North America indeed underscore the truth that affluence can be a greater threat to the vitality of faith than bloody persecution and open affliction.

What about the "great tribulation" spoken of in the Olivet discourse (Matt. 24:21; Mark 13:19; Luke 21:23)? The position taken here is that Jesus in this section of the discourse (Matt. 24:15-26) is referring specifically to the devastation of Jerusalem in A.D. 70 by the armies of the Roman general Titus.[16] In verses 1-2 of this chapter Jesus specifically refers to the destruction of the temple. The references to the holy place, Judea, and the sabbath (vv. 15-16, 20) clearly identify the location of the tribulation as Judea (v. 21), and more specifically, Jerusalem. In his parallel treatment of the Olivet discourse Luke makes it especially clear that the tribulation spoken of refers to God's judgment upon the unbelieving Jews: "For great distress shall be upon the earth [or, land; *ges*] and wrath *upon this people*" (21:23, italics added).

It might be thought that the specific language of Matthew 24:21, "great tribulation, *such as has not been from the*

---

[16] For this approach, see also J. Marcellus Kik, *An Eschatology of Victory* (Nutley, N.J.: Presbyterian and Reformed, 1971); William Kimball, *The Great Tribulation* (1983; Grand Rapids: Baker, 1984); William Barclay, "Matthew 24," *Expository Times* 70 (1959): 326-30; Ray Summers, "Matthew 24-25: An Exposition," *Review and Expositor* 59 (1962): 501-11.

beginning of the world until now, no, and *never will be"* (italics added), could not possibly have found its fulfillment in A.D. 70. Specific knowledge concerning the siege of Jerusalem will modify this impression, however. "The final siege and fall of Jerusalem form one of the most terrible stories in all history," writes William Barclay.[17]

According to the Jewish historian Josephus, ninety-seven thousand Jews were taken captive by the Romans, and more than one million died during the siege by the sword or by slow starvation. Josephus describes the progress of the siege: "Then did the famine widen its progress, and devoured the people by whole houses and families; the upper rooms were full of women and children that were dying of famine; and the lanes of the city were full of the dead bodies of the aged; the children also and the young men wandered about the market-places like shadows, all swelled with the famine, and fell down dead wheresoever their misery seized them. As for burying them, those that were sick themselves were not able to do it; and those that were hearty and well were deterred from doing it by the great multitude of those dead bodies, and by the uncertainty there was how soon they should die themselves, for many died as they were burying others, and many went to their coffins before the fatal hour was come" (*Wars of the Jews,* 5.12.3). One woman was driven to such desperation during the siege that she killed, roasted, and ate her nursing child (6.3.4). Even the Romans were horrified when they entered the city and saw the conditions within: When the Romans "were come to the houses to plunder them, they found in them entire families of dead men, and the upper rooms full of dead corpses . . . they then stood in horror of this sight, and went out without touching anything" (6.8.5).

More Jews were killed in the Holocaust, but in the intensity and quality of the suffering, the siege of Jerusalem

[17] Barclay, "Matthew 24," p. 327.

would appear to be unparalleled in recorded history. Indeed, God's wrath for all the righteous blood spilled on earth fell upon that generation (Matt. 23:36), as Christ had predicted. It is true that Revelation 7:14 speaks of saints who come out of the great tribulation, but nowhere is it stated that this is a period specific to the end time. Tribulation is indeed an experience of saints throughout church history, as John himself attests: "I John, your brother . . . share with you in Jesus the tribulation and the kingdom" (Rev. 1:9). The "great tribulation" of Matthew 24:21, however, does not refer to a final worldwide, violent persecution immediately prior to the second advent, but rather to God's judgment in Jerusalem in A.D. 70.

"When the Son of Man Comes, Will He Find Faith on Earth?"

There are not only those texts that have been taken to imply a steady deterioration of conditions in the world with the passage of time; there are also those that appear to predict decline in the church as well. The text already cited (Luke 18:8) is one such passage, and there are others in the New Testament. In the Sermon on the Mount, Christ tells the crowds that "the gate is narrow and the way is hard, that leads to life, and those who find it are few" (Matt. 7:14; cf. Luke 13:24, "Strive to enter by the narrow door"). Christ also stated that "many are called, but few are chosen" (Matt. 22:14). Can such texts he reconciled with the picture of vast numbers of people being converted to the Christian faith during a future period of great revival?

With respect to Luke 18:8, "when the Son of man comes, will he find faith on earth," it should be recalled that the postmillennial framework does recognize a period of apostasy and decline immediately prior to the parousia (Rev.

20:7-8; cf. 2 Thess. 2:1-11). It is to this period that Luke 18:8 is understood to refer. The preceding context (Luke in 17:22-37) speaks of the complacency and carelessness that will be characteristic of society immediately prior to the end, and by implication Christ warns the disciples not to become infected by this worldly spirit.

In his commentary on this text, Frederic Godet writes that we "must here remember the sad picture of the state of humanity at this epoch (17:26-30). Is it not to such a state of things that Jesus also makes allusion, Matt[hew] 25:5: 'And they *all* slumbered and slept?'"[18]

The period of apostasy immediately prior to the parousia, which will threaten to engulf even the faithful in spiritual complacency (Luke 18:8; Matt. 25:5), does not exclude a period of great revival before the final falling away. Indeed, the great revival of the church, and its secondary effects in particular-temporal peace and material prosperity (cf. Isa. 2:2-4; 65:20-25) are the conditions that make the warnings about spiritual complacency so relevant. The saying in Luke 18:8 warns the believers to not let their faith waver, notwithstanding the apparent delay in the return of Christ,[19] and despite the spirit of worldliness around them (17:26-30).

The sayings concerning the narrow gate (Matt. 7:14), the narrow door (Luke 13:24), and the few who are chosen (Matt. 22:14) are best understood in the context of Jesus' own earthly ministry.[20] The "gate" or "door" that leads to eternal life is narrow in several respects. First, it is narrow theologically: Jesus, and Jesus alone, is the door to eternal life (John 10:7,

---

[18] Frederic Godet, *A Commentary of the Gospel of St. Luke,* trans. M. D. Cusin, 5th ed., 2 vols. (reprint ed., Edinburgh: T. and T. Clark, 1976), vol. 2, pp. 202-3.

[19] Norval Geldenhuys, *Commentary on the Gospel of Luke* (Grand Rapids: Eerdmans, 1981), p. 447

[20] See Benjamin B. Warfield, "Are They Few that Be Saved?" in *Biblical and Theological Studies,* ed. Samuel G. Craig (Philadelphia: Presbyterian and Reformed, 1952), pp. 334-50.

"I am the door of the sheep"). The others who came before Christ are thieves and robbers (John 10:8) - false prophets and messianic pretenders such as Theudas and Judas theGalilean (Acts 5:36,37) - who lead the sheep astray. "There is salvation in no one else but Christ, and there is no other name under heaven given among men by which we must be saved" (Acts 4:12).

Second, the "gate" is narrow circumstantially in that few of the Jews responded savingly to the Lord's own earthly ministry; indeed, he was "despised and rejected by men" (Isa. 53:3). Many of the Jews were called to the messianic banquet (Matt. 22:14; also read vv. 1-13), but relatively few responded to the Lord himself.

These sayings (Matt. 7:14; Luke 13:24; Matt. 22:14), then, must be seen against the backdrop of the limited response of Israel to Christ's Palestinian ministry. They are not intended to settle the issue of the ultimate outcome and magnitude of Christ's redemptive work. The parables of the mustard seed and the leaven (Matt. 13:31-33) indeed show that over the course of time Jesus expected remarkable growth for the kingdom. The apostle Paul, who is disappointed by the limited response of the Jews of his own day, foresees a time when "all Israel will be saved" (Rom. 11:26). John of the Apocalypse writes to churches facing persecution and martyrdom, but is given the vision of a countless multitude of the redeemed standing before Christ's throne at the end of time (Rev. 7:9). Such texts help us to see Matthew 7:14, Luke 13:24, and Matthew 22:14 in the proper perspective, and prevent us from drawing pessimistic conclusions concerning the ultimate results of Christ's redemptive work.

FIVE

Summary and Conclusions

It is now time to attempt to draw together the various lines of argument that have been presented and to consider some implications for the mission of the church and its ministry. The major themes of the preceding chapters may be briefly summarized as follows:

1. Postmillennialism is an eschatological outlook that anticipates a period of unprecedented revival in the church prior to the return of Christ, resulting from new outpourings of the Holy Spirit. This great revival is expected to be characterized by the church's numerical expansion and spiritual vitality. As a secondary result of the growing influence of Christian values, the world as a whole is expected to experience conditions of significant peace and economic improvement. This postmillennial expectation is not to be confused with notions of secular progress, faith in science and technology, a myth of inevitable progress, the social gospel, or "manifest destiny." The postmillennial outlook as here understood is grounded fundamentally in Christology—in the vision of the victorious reign of the resurrected and ascended Lord at the right hand of the Father, who is actively extending the kingdom of God in the world through the power of his Word and Spirit. It is also noted that this general understanding of biblical eschatology was the dominant view among conservative Protestants for much of the nineteenth century. Its adherents have included such notable con-

servative theologians as John Owen, Jonathan Edwards, Charles Hodge, Robert L. Dabney, A. H. Strong, Benjamin B. Warfield, and others.

2. The expansive nature of God's redemptive purposes in the Old Testament is seen with particular clarity in the Abrahamic covenant and in the messianic promises and prophecies. In the Abrahamic covenant God reveals his purpose to ultimately bring spiritual blessings to all the families of the earth (Gen. 12:3). Abraham is challenged to believe that his spiritual descendants will be as numberless as the stars of heaven (Gen. 15:5-6) and as the sand on the seashore (Gen. 22:17). In subsequent Old Testament revelation it becomes clear that God's Messiah will be instrumental in bringing these universal blessings into history. Messianic psalms such as Psalms 2, 22, 72, and 110 depict a great king, God's Messiah, ruling over a vast kingdom that far transcends the boundaries of the nation Israel. This future messianic kingdom is also foreshadowed in the prophets. Isaiah 2:2-4 depicts a latter-day glory for the church, the spiritual Zion. Isaiah 9:6-7 speaks of the increasing reign of the new Davidic king, a prophecy whose fulfillment was initiated with the ascension of Christ to the right hand of the Father (Acts 2:30-31, 33-35). The peaceful conditions of the messianic reign in history are also spoken of in Isaiah 11:6-10 and 65:17-25. Ezekiel's vision of the miraculous life-giving river issuing from the temple, bringing new life and vitality to the desert (Ezek. 47:1-12), is understood to foreshadow the great outpouring of the Spirit that was initiated at Pentecost (cf. John 7:37-39), but not terminated by that event. Daniel's vision of the mysterious stone from heaven that strikes the image and becomes a great mountain filling the whole earth (Dan. 2:31-35) is a picture of the victorious kingdom of Jesus Christ, overcoming all worldly opposition and spreading throughout the earth. Daniel's vision of the heavenly Son of man, who is presented before the Ancient of Days (Dan. 7:13-14), depicts the reception of the ascended Christ by the Father in

heaven and Christ's universal reign over the world from the right hand of God. These promises of the Abrahamic covenant and the messianic texts point forward in time to the New Testament's Great Commission (Matt. 28:19-20), where the church in its mission is the instrument through which the risen Christ in heaven progressively extends his lordship over the nations.

3. The examination of the New Testament data is organized along the following lines: first, texts pointing to the greatness of Christ the King; second, texts describing the growth of Christ's kingdom; and third, texts highlighting the final greatness of Christ's kingdom. Passages such as Matthew 28:18 and Ephesians 1:19-23 attest to the unlimited authority of the ascended Christ, a spiritual authority available to the church in its mission. The parables of growth (Matt. 12:31-33) show the dramatic growth of the kingdom from insignificant beginnings and its quiet but pervasive impact on the world. The spiritual weapons of the church's warfare have divine power to destroy strongholds (2 Cor. 10:3-5). Christ actively subdues his foes while reigning from the Father's right hand in heaven, a victorious process culminating in the overthrow of death itself at the parousia and final resurrection (1 Cor. 15:22-26). The final greatness of Christ's kingdom is foreshadowed in texts such as Revelation 7:9-10, where John speaks of a great multitude of the redeemed that no man can number. The apostle Paul looks forward to a time when the fullness of ethnic Israel will be saved (Rom. 11:25-26). The closing pages of the New Testament contain a magnificent picture of the New Jerusalem (Rev. 21:15-16), a vast city covering some 2,250,000 square miles—a powerful image of the vastness of God's saving purposes.

4. Texts which appear to be at variance with the postmillennial outlook are examined. Passages indicating the imminency of the parousia (e.g., 1 Cor. 7:29; James 5:9; 1 Peter 4:7; 1 John 2:18; Rev. 22:20) are understood

christologically and pneumatologically, rather than in a merely chronological sense. In the death and resurrection of Christ, the events of the end time have already been inaugurated, and through the presence of the Holy Spirit, the believing church experiences even now the reality and power of Christ's victory that will in the future be visibly manifested to the world. The "great tribulation" (Matt. 24:21) is taken to be the destruction of Jerusalem in A.D. 70 by the Roman armies of Titus. The church experiences times of tribulation throughout history (John 16:33), but tribulation does not imply defeat, for Christ has overcome the world. Christ's sayings concerning the narrow door and the narrow gate (Matt. 7:13-14; Luke 13:23-24) describe the limited response of the Jews to the earthly ministry of Jesus, and not the ultimate outcome of God's saving purpose, described elsewhere (as in the parables of growth).

This reexamination of the postmillennial tradition has centered not on chronological speculations, date-setting, or readings of the "signs of the times," but rather on the biblical vision of the victorious kingdom of the resurrected and ascended Christ. Eschatology is seen to be fundamentally an outworking of Christology, and not a projected calendar of the future events. Given the biblical witness to the victory and present reign of Jesus Christ, the church can look to the future with realism and hope. The expansion of Christ's kingdom in history is marked by opposition, conflict, persecution, and temporary setbacks and defeats. The overall trend of history is clear, however. The mighty stone from heaven will overcome all worldly opposition and grow to fill the entire earth. This biblical vision can give today's church a tremendous impetus for its missionary and social task, as indeed it did to earlier generations of Christians. Today's church needs to turn its attention away from any preoccupations with worldly conditions in order to grasp anew, by faith, the magnificent vision of the mighty Christ at the Father's right hand who is Lord of lords and King of kings.

Christ the mighty King reigns *now*, and his invincible power is available to the church. It is in this hope that Christ's disciples can labor confidently and perseveringly for the extension of his kingdom in the world. "Hallelujah! For the Lord our God the Almighty reigns" (Rev. 19:6).

Bibliography

Books

Archer, Gleason L., Jr., trans. *Jerome's Commentary on Daniel*. Grand Rapids: Baker, 1958.

Barclay, William. *The Revelation of John*. 2 vols. Philadelphia: Westminster, 1976.

Barrett, C. K. *A Commentary on the First Epistle to the Corinthians*. New York: Harper and Row, 1968.

Barth, Markus. *The Broken Wall: A Study of the Epistle to the Ephesians*. Chicago: Judson, 1959.

Blackman, Philip, trans. *Mishnayoth*. 7 vols. New York: Judaica Press, 1963.

Boettner, Loraine. *The Millennium*. Philadelphia: Presbyterian and Reformed, 1957.

Boutflower, Charles. *In and Around the Book of Daniel*. Grand Rapids: Zondervan, 1963.

Bratcher, Robert G. *A Translator's Guide to the Gospel of Mark*. London: United Bible Societies, 1981.

Broadus, John A. *Commentary on the Gospel of Matthew.* Philadelphia: American Baptist Publication Society, 1886.

Brown, Raymond E. *The Epistles of John.* Garden City, N.Y.: Doubleday, 1982.

_____. *The Gospel According to John.* Garden City, N.Y.: Doubleday, 1966.

Bruce, F. F. *The Epistle of Paul to the Romans.* Grand Rapids: Eerdmans, 1963.

Calvin, John. *Commentaries on the First Book of Moses, Called Genesis.* Translated by John King. 2 vols. Grand Rapids: Eerdmans, 1948.

_____. *Commentary on the Book of the Prophet Isaiah.* Translated by William Pringle. 4 vols. Grand Rapids: Eerdmans, 1948.

_____. *Institutes of the Christian Religion.* Edited by John T. McNeill. Translated by Ford Lewis Battles. 2 vols. Philadelphia: Westminster, 1960.

_____. *The Second Epistle of Paul the Apostle to the Corinthians and the Epistles to Timothy, Titus, and Philemon.* Edited by David W. Torrance and Thomas F. Torrance. Translated by T. A. Smail. Grand Rapids: Eerdmans, 1964.

Cassuto, Umberto. *A Commentary on the Book of Genesis.* Translated by Israel Abrahams. 2 vols. Jerusalem: Magnes Press, 1964.

Chilton, David. *Paradise Restored.* Tyler, Tex.: American Bureau for Economic Research, 1984.

Conzelmann, Hans. *1 Corinthians: A Commentary on the First Epistle to the Corinthians.* Edited by George W. MacRae. Translated by James W. Leitch. Philadelphia: Fortress, 1975.

Davies, W. D. *Paul and Rabbinic Judaism.* London: S.P.C.K., 1955.

Dibelius, Martin, and Hans Conzelmann. *The Pastoral Epistles: A Commentary on the Pastoral Epistles.* Edited by Helmut Koester. Translated by Philip Buttolph and Adela Yarbro. Philadelphia: Fortress, 1972.

Easton, Burton Scott. *The Pastoral Epistles.* London: SCM, 1948.

Edwards, Jonathan. *Apocalyptic Writings.* Vol. 5 of The Works of Jonathan Edwards. Edited by Stephen J. Stein. New Haven: Yale University Press, 1977.

Erickson, Millard J. *Contemporary Options in Eschatology: A Study of the Millennium.* Grand Rapids: Baker, 1977.

Fonck, Leopold. *The Parables of the Gospel: An Exegetical and Practical Explanation.* New York: Frederick Pustet Co., 1914.

Foulkes, Francis. *The Epistle of Paul to the Ephesians: An Introduction and Commentary.* Grands Rapids: Eerdmans, 1963.

Geldenhuys, Norval. *Commentary on the Gospel of Luke.* Grand Rapids: Eerdmans, 1981.

Godet, Frederic. *A Commentary on the Gospel of St. Luke.* 5th ed. Translated by M. D. Cusin. 2 vols. Reprint ed. Edinburgh: T. and T. Clark, 1976.

Goodwin, Thomas. *An Exposition of Ephesians*. Reprint ed. Evansville, Ind.: Sovereign Grace Book Club, 1958.

Hammer, Raymond. *The Book of Daniel*. Cambridge: Cambridge University Press, 1976.

Hay, David M. *Glory at the Right Hand: Psalm 110 in Early Christianity*. Nashville: Abingdon, 1973.

Henry, Matthew. *Commentary on the Whole Bible*. Edited by Leslie F. Church. 1-vol. ed. Reprint ed. Grand Rapids: Zondervan, 1961.

Hering, Jean. *The First Epistle of Saint Paul to the Corinthians*. London: Epworth, 1962.

Hodge, Charles. *An Exposition of the Second Epistle to the Corinthians*. 1859. Grand Rapids: Baker, 1980.

_____. *Systematic Theology*. 3 vols. 1872-73. Grand Rapids: Eerdmans, 1968.

Kalt, Edmund, ed. *Herder's Commentary on the Psalms*. Translated by Bernard Fritz. Westminster, Md.: Newman Press, 1961.

Keil, K. F., and Franz Delitzsch. *Biblical Commentary on the Old Testament*. Translated by James Martin. 25 vols. *The Pentateuch*, 3 vols.; *The Psalms*, 3 vols.; *The Twelve Minor Prophets*, 2 vols. Grand Rapids: Eerdmans, 1949.

Kik, J. Marcellus. *An Eschatology of Victory*. Nutley, N.J.: Presbyterian and Reformed, 1971.

Kimball, William. *The Great Tribulation*. 1983. Grand Rapids: Baker, 1984.

Lacocque, Andre. *The Book of Daniel.* Translated by David Pellauer. Atlanta: John Knox, 1978.

Leenhardt, Franz J. *The Epistle to the Romans: A Commentary.* Translated by Harold Knight. Cleveland: World, 1961.

Lenski, R. C. H. *The Interpretation of St. John's Revelation.* Minneapolis: Augsburg, 1961.

_____. *The Interpretation of St. Luke's Gospel.* Columbus, Ohio: Wartburg, 1946.

_____. *The Interpretation of St. Matthew's Gospel.* Columbus, Ohio: Wartburg, 1943.

_____. *The Interpretation of St. Paul's Epistle to the Romans.* Minneapolis: Augsburg, 1961.

_____. *The Interpretation of St. Paul's First and Second Epistles to the Corinthians.* Minneapolis: Augsburg, 1961.

Lightfoot, J. B. *Saint Paul's Epistles to the Colossians and to Philemon.* London: Macmillan, 1882.

Moore, A. L. *The Parousia in the New Testament.* Leiden: E. J. Brill, 1966.

Morris, Leon. *The First and Second Epistles to the Thessalonians.* Grand Rapids: Eerdmans, 1959.

Mounce, Robert H. *The Book of Revelation.* Grand Rapids: Eerdmans, 1977.

Mowinkel, Sigmund. *He That Cometh: The Messiah Concept in the Old Testament and Later Judaism.* Translated by G. W. Anderson. New York: Abingdon, 1956.

Owen, John. *The Works of John Owen*. Edited by William H. Goold. 16 vols. 1850. London: Banner of Truth, 1967.

Perowne, J. J. Stewart. *The Book of Psalms*. 2 vols. Andover: Warren F. Draper, 1894.

Rad, Gerhard von. *Genesis: A Commentary*. Translated by John H. Marks. Philadelphia: Westminster, 1961.

Russell, J. Stuart. *The Parousia: A Study of the New Testament Doctrine of Our Lord's Second Coming*. Reprint ed. Grand Rapids: Baker, 1983.

Schaff, Philip, ed. *The Creeds of Christedom*. 6th ed. 3 vols. Reprint ed. Grand Rapids: Baker, 1983.

Smith, Timothy L. *Revivalism and Social Reform in Mid-Nineteenth-Century America*. Nashville: Abingdon, 1957.

Toon, Peter, ed. *Puritans, the Millennium and the Future of Israel: Puritan Eschatology 1600 to 1660*. Cambridge: James Clark, 1970.

Trench, Richard C. *Notes on the Parables of Our Lord*. New York: N. Tibbals and Sons, 1879.

Warfield, Benjamin Breckinridge. *Biblical and Theological Studies*. Edited by Samuel G. Craig. Philadelphia: Presbyterian and Reformed, 1952.

Young, Edward J. *The Book of Isaiah*. 3 vols. Grand Rapids: Eerdmans, 1965.

Zimmerli, Walther. *Ezekiel 2*. Philadelphia: Fortress, 1983.

Articles

Bahnsen, Greg. "The Prima Facie Acceptability of Postmillenialism." *Journal of Christian Reconstruction* 3:2 (1976-77): 48-105.

Barclay, William. "Matthew 24." *Expository Times* 70 (1959): 326-30.

Baukham, Richard J. "The Delay of the Parousia." *Tyndale Bulletin* 31 (1980): 3-36.

Beasley-Murray, G .R. "The Interpretation of Daniel 7." *Catholic Biblical Quarterly* 45:1 (1983): 44-58.

Beckwith, Clarence Augustine. "The Millennium." *The New Schaff-Herzog Encyclopedia of Religious Knowledge*, edited by Samuel Macauley Jackson. Vol. 7. New York: Funk and Wagnalls, 1910.

Clouse, Robert G. "Millennium, Views of the." *Evangelical Dictionary of Theology*, edited by Walter A. Elwell. Grand Rapids: Baker, 1984.

Davies, J. G. "The Genesis of Belief in an Immanent Parousia." *Journal of Theological Studies* n.s. 14 (1963): 104-7.

Di Lella, Alexander A. "The One in Human Likeness and the Holy Ones of the Most High in Daniel 7." *Catholic Biblical Quarterly* 39:1 (1977): 1-19.

Granata, G. "La 'sinapis' del Vangelo." *Bibliotheca Orientalis* 24 (1982): 175-77.

Grigsby, Bruce. "Gematria and John 21:11: Another Look at Ezekiel 47:10." *Expository Times* 95:6 (1984): 177-78.

Gundrey, Stanley N. "Hermeneutics or *Zeitgeist* as the Determining Factor in the History of Eschatologies?" *Journal of the Evangelical Theological Society* 20:1 (1977): 45-55.

Hiers, Richard H. "The Delay of the Parousia in Luke-Acts." *New Testament Studies* 20 (1974): 145-55.

Horne, Charles M. "The Meaning of the Phrase, 'And Thus All Israel Will Be Saved' (Rom. 11:26)." *Evangelical Theological Society Journal* 21 (1978): 329-34.

Lambrecht, J. "Paul's Christological Use of Scripture in 1 Cor. 15:20-28." *New Testament Studies* 28 (1982): 502-27.

Loader, W. R. G. "Christ at the Right Hand--Ps. 110:1 in the New Testament." *New Testament Studies* 24 (1978): 199-217.

Longenecker, Richard N. "The Nature of Paul's Early Eschatology." *New Testament Studies* 31 (1985): 85-95.

McArthur, Harvey K. "The Parable of the Mustard Seed." *Catholic Biblical Quarterly* 33 (1971): 198-210.

MacRae, George W. "The Meaning and Evolution of the Feast of Tabernacles." *Catholic Biblical Quarterly* 22 (1960): 251-76.

Moorhead, James H. "The Erosion of Postmillennialism in American Religious Thought, 2865-1925." *Church History* 53:1 (1984): 61-77.

Owen, H. P. "The Parousia of Christ in the Synoptic Gospels." *Scottish Journal of Theology* 12 (1959): 171-92.

Pace, G. "La senepa del Vangelo." *Bibliotheca Orientalis* 22 (1980): 119-23.

Quandt, Jean B. "Religion and Social Thought: The Secularization of Postmillennialism." *American Quarterly* 25 (1973): 390-409.

Smith, Timothy L. "Righteousness and Hope: Christian Holiness and the Millennial Vision in America, 1800-1900." *American Quarterly* 31:1 (1979): 21-45.

Sproule, J. A. "The Problem of the Mustard Seed." *Grace Theological Journal* 1 (1980): 37-42.

Summers, Ray. "Matthew 24-25: An Exposition." *Review and Expositor* 59 (1962): 501-11.

Talbert, Charles H. "II Peter and the Delay of the Parousia." *Vigilae Christianae* 20 (1966): 137-45.

Wallis, W. B. "The Problem of an Intermediate Kingdom in 1 Corinthians 15:20-28." *Evangelical Theological Society Journal* 18 (1975): 229-42.